R-4207-USDP

Indian Strategic Thought

An Interpretive Essay

George K. Tanham

Prepared for the
Under Secretary of Defense for Policy

PREFACE

This report was prepared by the RAND project entitled "India's Future Strategic Role and Power Potential" under the International Security and Defense Strategy Program of RAND's National Defense Research Institute, a federally funded research and development center sponsored by the Office of the Secretary of Defense and the Joint Staff. The project, sponsored by the Office of the Under Secretary of Defense for Policy, assessed: (1) the historical and cultural factors that have shaped Indian strategic thinking; (2) the evolving lines of security debate within the Indian civilian and military leadership; (3) the technical, economic, and institutional factors affecting the evolution of Indian military power; and (4) the longer-term implications of India's regional security role for the United States.

The present study focuses on the historical, geographic, and cultural factors influencing Indian strategic thinking: how India's past has shaped present-day conceptions of military power and national security; how Indian elites view their strategic position vis-à-vis their neighbors, the Indian Ocean, and great power alignments; whether Indian thinking follows a reasonably consistent logic and direction; and what this might imply for India's long-term capability to shape its regional security environment.

The report attempts to distill the enduring themes of Indian strategic policies as gathered in numerous conversations with Indians in India and the United States, wide reading, and observation of Indian behavior. Other RAND publications will explore in greater detail the evolution of Indian security policy since independence and the pace and directions of India's military modernization effort. The report should be of interest to policymakers responsible for regional security planning, especially that related to South Asia.

SUMMARY

India does not admit easily to broad generalizations. It is an extraordinarily complex and diverse society, and Indian elites show little evidence of having thought coherently and systematically about national strategy, although this situation may now be changing. Despite India's cultural greatness and longevity as a civilization, Indian history is often dimly perceived and poorly recorded; given an oral tradition in imparting past events and the destruction of most records, much of this history is difficult to verify. Until the middle of the eighteenth century, Indians knew little of their national history and seemed uninterested in it.

Few writings offer coherent, articulated beliefs or a clear set of operating principles for Indian strategy. Rather, one finds a complex mix of writings, commentaries, and speeches, as well as certain actions that cast some light on Indian strategy. The lacunae and ambiguities seem compatible with a culture that encompasses and accommodates readily to complexity and contradiction. They also seem more confusing to Westerners than to Indians, who accept the complexities and contradictions as part of life.

Four principal factors help to explain Indian actions and views about power and security: Indian geography; the "discovery" of Indian history by Indian elites over the past 150 years; Indian cultural and social structures and belief systems; and the British rule (raj).

Geography has imparted a view of the Indian subcontinent as a single strategic entity, with various topographical features contributing to an insular perspective and a tradition of localism and particularism. India's unique culture reinforced this unity and imparted, first, a tendency toward diversity and accommodation to existing realities and, second, a highly developed capacity to absorb dissimilar concepts and theories. This tolerance was strengthened by the caste system, which also helped maintain an extraordinarily durable system and ethic for social relations.

The discovery of history underscores the primacy of culture in India's political development and world outlook. Brief periods of imperial unity strengthened the notions of an old and great India and provided rare examples of its political unity. In the fourth and third centuries BC, indigenous leaders, the Mauryans, created an early model of national unity; in the tenth century AD, invaders, the Moghuls, provided imperial leadership.

Thus, the assumed superiority of Indian culture became a continuing thread running through Indian history, enabling India to accommodate to powerful foreign forces that were far more purposeful in the exercise of military power. Culture also provided the basis for an Indian identity. At the same time, Indians have exhibited little taste for conquest or expansion beyond the subcontinent.

Finally, the experience of the British raj provided India with a geopolitical frame of reference that continues to influence present-day Indian strategy. As the British built and nurtured their empire in India, they also evolved a strategy for India's defense. On land and sea, the British sought to deny other powers easy access to the subcontinent. They set up buffer states to secure the land periphery and help defend the core; sea control ensured that all other powers were denied the means to penetrate Indian waters or to challenge any strategic sea routes.

Progressively, but inescapably, Indian leaders since independence have assumed the mantle of the British raj. In the aftermath of the partition of the subcontinent, the ascendance of a unified Chinese state, the step-by-step withdrawal of British power east of Suez, and an increasing American presence in the Indian Ocean, postindependence Indians have felt vulnerable and surrounded, though neither is a new sensation for India.

At the same time, Jawaharlal Nehru, India's first prime minister, pursued nonalignment as an international strategy, hoping to avoid Indian entrapment in great-power rivalries and to enable India to focus on internal development. Rivalry with the Chinese and the Chinese attack of 1962, however, eroded and ultimately shattered Nehru's vision.

Over time, a set of policies and strategies evolved informally to deal with the complex strategic dilemmas related to internal unity and potential threats from abroad. These strategies, which placed India at the center of a series of concentric geographical circles or rings, sought to

- Prevent any of India's small neighbors from recourse to foreign policy actions or solicitation of external support deemed inimical to Indian interests.

- Encourage the development of capabilities to (1) deny Pakistan a meaningful potential to challenge Indian predominance on the sub-continent and (2) deter or defeat hostile Pakistani actions.
- Obtain the resources to (1) fight a two-front war, thereby keeping any potential Chinese challenge to Indian security at bay, and (2) achieve symbolic "power equivalence" with China.
- Achieve close relations with the Soviet Union to counter China and Pakistan.
- Develop naval capabilities that (1) could deny any extraregional power from achieving a meaningful naval presence in the Indian Ocean and (2) would give India superiority over any combination of local navies, thereby seeking legitimacy for Indian predominance in the Indian Ocean.
- Approach world-power status by developing nuclear and missile capabilities, a blue-water navy, and a military-industrial complex, all obvious characteristics of the superpowers; yet recognition as a great world nation (rather than as a superpower) was the paramount goal.

Some general characteristics and objectives of Indian strategy emerge from the above evolution. India has developed a predominantly defensive strategic orientation. Its large ground forces remain defensive and protective, although some leaders now seek a more offensively oriented strategy. Military technology seems to be pointing India in this direction. It remains a largely land-oriented nation, with the greatest effort and money going first to the Army and second to the Air Force. The Navy, largely defensive in strategic design, is gradually developing sea-denial capabilities; a few advocates seek some power-projection capability.

India retains a long-term, unshakable commitment to strategic independence and autonomy in its decisionmaking and military capabilities, although its economic, industrial, and technological shortcomings continue to limit the success of such a strategic design. It wants to play the role of peacekeeper in the Indian Ocean and to be recognized in that role by the great powers. It hopes, through these and other efforts, ultimately to achieve acceptance (perhaps especially by the United States) of its status as a global power.

At the same time, however, the Indian government has not succeeded in articulating or pursuing these goals in a coherent, disciplined fashion. Some of the directions of recent Indian military development (especially the enhancement of naval capabilities) have yet to be systematically assessed or presented. Some circles reveal ambivalence about the implications of any decision to pursue authoritatively and unambiguously a declared nuclear weapons capability.

Indians also realize now that the high technology being developed for India's longer-term defense has implications for Indian strategy, but these have not been thought out. Also, domestic and budgetary constraints will clearly continue to limit the growth and exercise of Indian military power for many years to come, though most Indians agree on the need for strong military forces. At least some Indian elites believe that acquisition of modern capabilities will remain critical to assuring the nation an international position commensurate with its history, aspirations, and ambitions.

ACKNOWLEDGMENTS

First, I would like to thank Stephen P. Cohen for encouraging me at the start of this project, for generously sharing his knowledge and understanding of India, and for helping me with the draft of this report. Jonathan Pollack gave strong support to my work and also carefully reviewed the draft providing helpful and constructive criticism. Stephen T. Hosmer has been helpful particularly in organizing the report.

Scores of Indians assisted and encouraged me with my research. I want to thank them all for their generous help, kind understanding, and patience with a newcomer to India. I particularly want to thank Admiral K. K. Nayyar, who arranged many interviews and generously shared his firsthand knowledge of the Indian defense community, and P. K. Singh, formerly Joint Secretary of External Affairs and now the Indian Ambassador to Greece, for helping me launch the project in India, for arranging meetings, and assisting in many, many ways. Mrs. Mitra Vasisht of the Ministry of External Affairs has been most helpful in Delhi and Washington and has provided a constructive critique of the report.

Dr. K. Subrahmahyam gave most generously of his time and knowledge and patiently explained many facets of the strategic culture, especially the role of the Army. General Krishnaswami Sundarji was especially generous and forthcoming in his help. Admiral M. K. Roy assisted me directly and arranged several very useful seminars. Jasjit Singh was most helpful in sharing his knowledge and views. V. P. Venkateswaren patiently tried to explain Hinduism and Indian culture as a backdrop for Indian strategic culture.

Many other Indians have helped me: among them, Bhabani Sen Gupta, Raja Mohan, Eric Gonsalves, Giri Deshinker, M. Dubey, Prakash Shah, Lt. Gen. Matthew Thomas (Ret.), Vice Admiral S. Govil, Lt. Gen. V. K. Sood (Ret.), Lt. Gen. M. L. Chibber (Ret.), Maj. Gen. G. K. Bhimaya (Ret.), Lt. Gen. J.F.R. Jacob (Ret.), Maj. Gen. S. C. Singh (Ret.), Maj. Gen. D. Banerjee, R. R. Subramanian, Surjit Mansingh, V. P. Dutt, H. K. Dua, Capt. Bharat Verma (Ret.), Giri Lal Jain, Brigadier B. K. Nair (Ret.), and Capt. C. U. Bhaskar. Many others have helped, and I hope they also will accept my thanks.

In the Indian Embassy in Washington, Ambassador Lalit Mansingh, the DCM, and Brigadier Sen Gupta, the Defense Attaché, were most helpful. The former political counselor, Raminder Jassal, was extremely helpful and encouraging.

The two technical reviewers of this report, Leo Rose of the University of California and Gordon McCormick of RAND, provided incisive criticism and helpful suggestions.

To all these people my grateful thanks and deep appreciation. For the shortcomings and mistakes I alone am responsible.

CONTENTS

FIGURES

1. INFLUENCES ON INDIAN STRATEGIC THINKING

Since it gained independence from Britain in August 1947 and began to assume a more prominent place in the international community, India has groped to define and articulate a coherent strategic identity. Deeply embedded habits of thought related to India's geography, history, culture, and British rule exert a powerful influence on the character and directions of the modern Indian state; they will in the foreseeable future help to shape its strategic thinking and its strategy.

Now on its own for the first time in centuries, India is undergoing a wrenching transition between its traditional culture and the practices and influences of the modern world. The crosscurrents of India's past continually converge on the present. An Indian intellectual remarked that one can stand in New Delhi and observe the simultaneous existence of many centuries of Indian history. One cannot, however, foresee which elements of the past will persist and which new characteristics will penetrate the national ethos.

Ethnic, linguistic, religious, caste, and internal regional rivalries on a scale unimaginable to most Americans seem at times to prevail over national concerns and to threaten India's fragile coherence and national integration. At the same time, Indians appear consumed by personal and regional competition for political power—competition that diminishes India's claims to greatness and ambitions to play a larger international role.

The extraordinary diversity, the size of the country, and the dynamics of change sometimes make consensus over major issues difficult to achieve, and perhaps even more difficult to predict. Nevertheless, although the process is discontinuous and uneven, rapid economic, technological, and social innovations are changing the fabric of Indian society and its ways of thinking.

After a word on methodology, the remainder of this section discusses the four factors—geography, history, culture, and British rule (or raj)—that have most influenced the character and direction of modern Indian strategy and what thinking has been undertaken. Section 2 deals with Indian strategy as the Indians view it, and Section 3 analyzes the basis for India's relative lack of strategic thinking. Sections

4 and 5 touch briefly on the role of the Indian Army and India's nuclear ambitions.

The analysis is based on interviews and discussions with Indian intellectuals, government officials, and military strategists; observation of Indian actions in foreign policy and strategic affairs; and Indian historical and philosophical writings and the published sources listed in the bibliography.

This is an unusual project for RAND in that it attempts to investigate and report on how another people—the Indians—think about their own strategic matters. Literature on the subject is meager, and few persons inside or outside India have studied it or thought much about it. I began the research for this project by reading widely about India. Over the past four years, I made four trips to India, each over a month in length, during which I conducted a few structured interviews, but mostly engaged in informal conversations. These talks allowed Indians to express themselves easily and voluntarily on various subjects relevant to this study.

I called on many officials, including former foreign ministers, chiefs of the military services, and secretaries of defense and external affairs. I also spoke with academics, policy researchers, media personnel, businessmen, retired officials and military officers, and some average Indians. Most of the research was done in New Delhi, some in Bangalore, Madras, and Calcutta.

The report reflects primarily the viewpoints of what I call the Delhi nationalist elite, which I believe is the primary (though not the only) group concerned with strategy in India. The report does not fully represent the views of all of India, including the powerful regional personalities and pressures that can and do influence strategy and foreign policy.

I do not presume to understand India, but hope that I have acquired some limited insights into and understanding of Indian society and how it thinks about strategy and military matters. The results of my research follow.

GEOGRAPHY

Geography has profoundly affected India's history and culture and therefore its strategic thinking and strategy. Perhaps even more important than geography itself has been the conscious and often unconscious attitudes and thought processes that geography has induced in the formulation of Indian strategy. India's strategic location, size, and tremendous population have contributed to Indian leaders' belief in its greatness, its preeminence in the Indian Ocean region, and its global importance.

The Himalayas and the Hindu Kush mountains in the north, the Bay of Bengal in the east, and the Arabian Sea in the west have created a giant natural entity often referred to as the Indian subcontinent (see Figure 1). This diamond-shaped landmass stretches over 3000 kilometers from the southernmost tip of India north to the Himalayas and roughly the same distance from east to west. India, by far the largest part of the subcontinent, covers over 3 million square kilometers. It is the second largest nation in the world in population, with about 850 million people.

On a map of the eastern hemisphere (see Figure 2), India appears to lie at the intersection of imaginary lines stretching from southern Africa to far northeastern Russia and from Australia to the United Kingdom. Thus, Indians have the impression that India is the middle of this great region, though in most ways it is not. India does, however, occupy a strategic position in relation to all the trade between Australia and Europe and between the Far East and the Middle East and Europe.[1]

Geography, especially rivers and mountains, has divided as well as unified the Indian subcontinent. The Vindhaya range forms a north-south divide (see Figure 1). To the north of it lies the great plain of the Indus and Ganges (Ganga) rivers, its fertile soil watered by the monsoons. These great rivers rushing out of the Himalayas make the northern plain the heartland of India. This rich agricultural area allowed the development of large kingdoms and often led to the domination of parts of the more fragmented south.[2]

Over the centuries, invaders from the north, attracted by the riches of India, brought new cultures which added to and gradually adapted to Indian thought and society. Most of the invaders came from lands untouched by the sea, giving the dominant north a strong strategic land orientation with little attention to the ocean.

---

[1]Given India's strategic position astride some of the world's major trade routes and its long coastline, one would have expected an extensive history of maritime and naval operations. Although India has participated actively in international trade and commerce for centuries, it has not played a major role in the purely maritime aspects of trade, i.e., sailing the ships.

[2]See Romila Thapar, *A History of India*, Vol. 1, Penguin Books, London, 1987, p. 21, for a brief but interesting discussion of the influences of geography on the north and south.

4

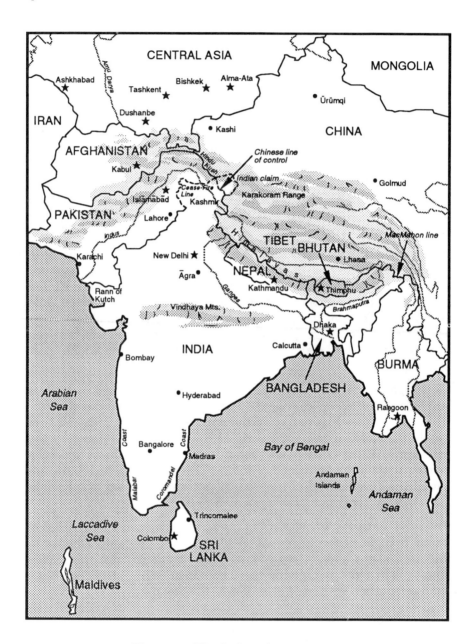

Figure 1—The Indian Subcontinent

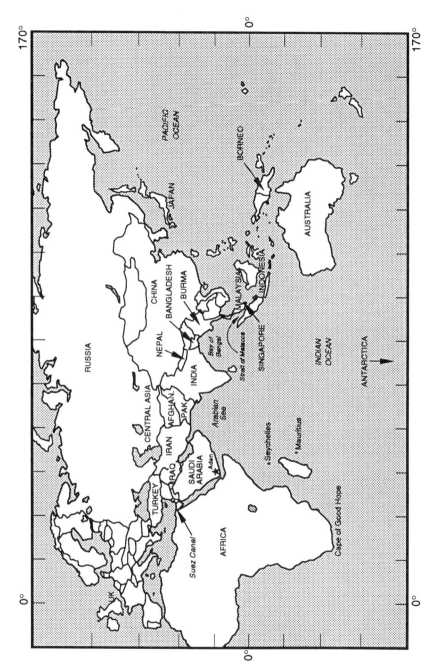

Figure 2—India in the Eastern Hemisphere

The south, occupied largely by peoples driven out of the Indian plain, was somewhat insulated from invaders and, thus, has retained more of its original Dravidian language and culture. Although the south is also agricultural, it has a much richer maritime tradition than the north. Parts of southern India, especially along the Malabar and Coromandel coasts, participated in the important commerce of the Indian Ocean, interacting by sea with the Arabs and Europeans to the west and the southeast Asians and Chinese to the east (see Figure 2, above).

These factors have contributed to a southern regionalism and a strategic outlook somewhat different from that of the north. Whereas northern India sees the threat from the northwest (today, Pakistan) and the north (China), the south resents the dominant northerners in India and looks seaward in its strategic approach.

Smaller rivers and lesser mountains have further divided India, especially in the south, and have created small geographical areas that developed separate entities with their own language, history, and local variation of the great Indian culture. Thus, geography has simultaneously unified and divided India, leading to its claim of unity with diversity and creating some of the tensions that plague India today.

Indians have long regarded the mountains and seas as protective barriers against outside interference and invasion. In fact, however, the passes in the northwest have allowed invaders over the centuries to overrun much of India. In World War II, the Japanese threatened India from the northeast, through Burma, and in 1962 the Chinese attacked across the mountains in the northwest and the northeast.

This dichotomy—the simultaneous sense of security based on geography and the realization that geography has failed to keep India secure—is partially offset by India's ability to accommodate in various ways to the invaders, thus creating and strengthening an evolving culture that plays a crucial role in modern India's identity. The dichotomy has, however, led to feelings of pride and confidence intermingled with feelings of insecurity and risk.

These same geographic barriers have played an even more important role in keeping Indians inside the subcontinent and allowing India to develop its own unique culture. In the view of Jawaharlal Nehru, India's first prime minister, India's "isolated evolution" is unique in the history of Indo-European peoples, although he acknowledges

India's widespread contact and relations with most of the external world while retaining its unique culture.[3]

Foreign visitors and scholars from both the East and the West have left useful accounts of early India. Traders from the Middle East, Europe, and China used India as a central staging area for their commerce. Until recent times, however, India has shown little interest in the outside world. Few historical accounts exist of Indians traveling abroad, and news of the outer world came mostly through foreigners. Thus, geography has strongly influenced Indian history and culture, both of which have centered on the subcontinent without great outside contact.

HISTORY

Indians' attempts in the nineteenth century to discover their history as a whole coincided with the growth of nationalism. Although this European concept was quite foreign to Indian views of political entities, its appearance at that particular time led many Indians to search for and interpret their history through the prism of nationalism.

Until the mid-nineteenth century, while Indians knew their own local history, they knew little of the history of India as a whole and seemed largely uninterested in it. In fact, some scholars have claimed that Indians were not interested in their history at all.[4] However, as discussed below, the Indian view of life and time are not conducive to a sense of history, at least in the Western style.[5]

In the eighteenth and nineteenth centuries, however, British administrators, Jesuits, and other Europeans became curious about the origins and history of the region referred to as India. Some of them learned Sanskrit and studied the sacred Vedic literature of the

---

[3]Jawaharlal Nehru, *The Discovery of India*, Oxford University Press, New Delhi, 1982, p. 88. According to Amaury de Riencourt, *The Soul of India*, rev., Honeyglen, UK, 1986, p. 152, "the sea played no part in the building of India" and India had "no organized relations with the oceans" as, for example, Southeast Asia had.

[4]de Riencourt (p. 15) says of Indians that "of all the people on earth they are the least interested in history." This statement applied less as nationalism developed. See also N. K. Sinha and Nisith R. Ray, *A History of India,* Orient Longman, Hyderabad, 1973, who maintain that Indians revere the past but know little of it (p. 10).

[5]India has few historical records and nothing comparable to the works of Herodotus or Thucydides in Greece in the fifth century BC. The Indian epics are great and moving accounts of certain historical events, but they are more mythology than history.

Aryans, the basis of at least Brahmanic Hinduism.[6] As Europeans uncovered and pieced together India's history and culture, they developed great respect for it. Indians also began to appreciate it, as they had never before viewed India from a complex perspective.

A renaissance of Hinduism, due in part to these historical discoveries, developed and blended with newfound nationalism, leading some Indians to develop a Hindu nationalism. However, Nehru and most Congress leaders preferred a secular nationalism and a secular state.

Because nationalism demanded deep historical roots, the Indian nationalists were among those most interested in the history of all of India, and they began to look for characteristics of the European nation state in their own history.[7] They were forced to go all the way back to the Mauryan empire of the fourth and third centuries BC to find a suitable example of an India governed by a central, indigenous ruling authority. The Mauryan empire, which covered almost all of India, had a vast and effective administrative structure that supported central authority and enhanced and encouraged loyalty to the emperor, though not to the state. The Mauryan empire was the exception, however, and did not establish a lasting precedent for Indian political unity.

The example of Ashoka, the great Mauryan emperor and a peaceful and moral leader, had a great effect on modern India. Indians pride themselves on the strong spiritual aspects and moral values of their society, and many nationalists found such qualities in Ashoka. When Ashoka, fighting for his empire, defeated his last opposition, the Kalingas, in an extremely bloody battle, he was so appalled by the slaughter that he decided to give up war.[8]

Ashoka later preached nonviolence, urged tolerance among groups, and tried to provide for the welfare of his subjects. Stone columns bearing inscriptions of exhortation and guidance for his subjects were discovered in the eighteenth century, but were not deciphered until

---

[6]Brahman here refers to the upper caste, rather than to Brahma, the world spirit. The Brahmans' more intellectual approach to Hinduism is called the Great Tradition; the less structured, more emotional, and more diverse approach is known as the Lesser Tradition. The Brahmans have carefully maintained the Great Tradition, which the English discovered before they encountered the Lesser Tradition. The latter, because it had innumerable variations and evolved orally, left a less clear and more diverse record.

[7]For a moving and inspirational example of one man's discovery of Indian history, see Nehru, 1982.

[8]Some cynics have argued that there was no one left to fight, but this seems doubtful: Local kings fought and eventually contributed to the end of the Mauryan empire.

the nineteenth. Ashoka himself was not positively identified as the great king until about 1915, but because he combined the attributes of strong leadership and high morality, he is now recognized as one of India's greatest national leaders. The Ashoka wheel of dharma (moral law) is now invested in the center of the Indian flag.

The search for other periods of political unity and great national leaders proved less fruitful. The Gupta dynasty of the fourth and fifth centuries AD produced able rulers who governed most of northern India, but their rule was less efficient and more limited in expanse than that of the Mauryan emperors.[9] Their reign is regarded as a golden age of Hinduism, however, when art, literature, and philosophy flourished. Though perhaps not as great as the Mauryan emperors, the Guptas are extremely important to those who consider Hinduism the essential element of Indian nationalism.[10]

Some 600 years later, beginning in the late tenth century, Muslim Turks from Afghanistan began to make raids into India. Only in the early sixteenth century, however, did the Muslim Moghuls, under Babur, begin to recreate a unified imperial state in South Asia. This new stability and order not only influenced India's own cultural development, but also led to Indian contributions to Islamic thought.[11] The Muslims brought new military technologies, a new theology, and new political ideas, but they did not destroy Indian civilization, as they had destroyed pre-Islamic Persian culture, nor did the Hindus completely absorb them. Islam in a sense became a second culture, though it did not entirely escape Indian influence.

Akbar, perhaps the greatest of the Moghul rulers, seeing the need to integrate the various communal divisions of India, tried, albeit unsuccessfully, to synthesize Hinduism and Islam. He lifted the taxes and restrictions laid on the Hindus by more zealous Muslim predecessors, consulted not only Hindus but Jews and Christians, and reportedly had Hindu, Jewish, and Christian wives. Many Hindus served

---

[9]Samudragupta (AD 320–380), probably the greatest Gupta emperor, has been called the "Indian Napoleon." See Lt. Col. H. C. Kar, *Military History of India,* Firma KLB Private Ltd., Calcutta, 1980, p. 69.

[10]The Indian nationalist movement in fact lost its cultural moorings and began "to coalesce with old Hindu xenophobia which had appeared before the Muslim conquest and became hardened under Muslim rule." See Nirad C. Chaudhuri, *Thy Hand, Great Anarch!* The Hogarth Press, London, 1987, p. 33.

[11]Many Middle Eastern fundamentalist groups have been influenced by the thought and writings of Abul Ala Maududi, who died in 1979 in Pakistan. Many ideas of the present Islamic revival came from India, and one of the most active *dahwah* (missionary) groups, the Indian Jamaat Tabligh, operates in parts of Southeast Asia, thus in a sense renewing Indian cultural ties to that area.

as military officers and administrators. Aurangzeb, Akbar's grandson and a more devout and strict Muslim, however, showed less tolerance and conciliation, thereby weakening the Moghul empire and arousing communal passions that still exist in India today.[12]

Not accidentally, many Indian leaders pursued tolerance through intermarriage or conversion. India is a dazzlingly diverse country, and no ruler or dynasty has been able to impose a single doctrine or ideology on its population. Chandra Gupta, the founder of the Mauryan dynasty, was a Hindu; his grandson Ashoka converted to Buddhism; the Guptas were Hindus; and the Moghuls were Muslims. Strikingly, Ashoka and Akbar—two non-Hindus—saw the need for tolerance and understanding among communal groups, though Hindus are noted for their tolerance.

Most of the modern Indian nationalist movement, especially the dominant Congress Party, accepted Hindu, Buddhist, and Muslim rulers as "Indians." That Indian nationalists accepted both Ashoka and Akbar is a tribute to their tolerance, pragmatism, and appreciation of greatness and also to their tradition of accepting and assimilating newcomers. Some nationalists, including Nehru, realized that the problems of integration that these emperors faced had continued into the twentieth century. For this reason, they opted for an independent secular state in which the different communal groups would be treated equally.

Two important dissents from this tradition of tolerance came during the period leading to independence. Segments of the Indian Muslim community felt that they could not live as a permanent minority in a predominantly Hindu state. This view eventually led to the movement for Pakistan. At the same time, a militant orthodox Hindu movement sought to make India a Hindu state. The Bharatya Janata Party (BJP) holds this position today and did well in the election of June 1991.

The nationalists searching for cohesion in India's past discovered, in addition to the short periods of national unity, the long periods of disunity. Geography had divided the country into small units, and these developed their own language and subculture, as well as traditions of political unity and separate identity. The modern nationalists saw throughout Indian history a tension between the factors working for unity and those perpetuating regionalism and disunity. Most of the

---

[12]Hindus see Aurangzeb as a fanatic and zealot, but Muslims insist that he was a stricter and more devout Muslim than Akbar.

time, the centrifugal forces seemed to dominate, at least in the political sphere. This powerful tradition of regionalism remains a formidable force to this day.

Thus, the discovery of India's political past, even through nationalist eyes, did not suffice to satisfy the needs of a vital nationalism. The infrequency of India's great and glorious empires only dramatized the absence of a lasting political unity. The nationalists therefore turned to the one continuous, powerful element in Indian history: its Hindu culture. The more deeply they delved into it, the prouder they became.[13]

Over several millennia, the Brahmanic tradition, with its sophisticated thought, its wide appeal, and its pervasiveness in Indian society, provided important cohesiveness to India's cultural continuity. For the Hindu nationalists, India had existed for several thousand years. Nehru movingly summarizes some of these thoughts and reflects his pride and excitement in *The Discovery of India:*

> The diversity of India is tremendous; it is obvious; it lies on the surface and nobody can see it. Yet, with all these differences, there is no mistaking the impress of India on the Pathan, as this is obvious on the Tamil. . . . Ancient India, like ancient China, was a world in itself, a culture and a civilization which gave shape to all things. Foreign influences poured in and often influenced that culture and were absorbed. Disruptive tendencies gave rise immediately to an attempt to find a synthesis. Some kind of a dream of unity has occupied the mind of India since the dawn of civilization. That unity was not conceived as something imposed from outside. . . . It was something deeper and, within its fold, the widest tolerance of belief and custom was practised and every variety acknowledged and even encouraged.[14]

This concept of national unity has translated into a special feeling of transcendent *Indianness*. Indianness implies more than political na-

---

[13]Some Indians have dismissed the nationalist leaders' knowledge of India and its cultural history. Chaudhuri (p. 33) wrote: "From 1921 onwards the nationalist movement was carried on in a growing cultural void. The civilization of ancient India became a subject of chauvinistic bragging. Hinduism, which was certainly the most stable, deep-rooted and authentic cultural force among a great majority of Indians, became in the Westernized India a nationalistic myth." The subsection immediately following, entitled "Culture," presents a brief overview of Hinduism as it relates to strategy.

[14]Jawaharlal Nehru, *The Discovery of India,* 4th ed., rev., Meridian Books, London, 1960, p. 49. Chaudhuri (p. 32) claims that Nehru knew little of India or its history.

tionalism; it is an emotion or belief based on cultural identity; it is the deep, intense feeling of being an Indian.[15]

Asked the meaning of Indianness, Indians give various answers, all based on culture. Some say that they can go to a different region of India with a different language and feel at home because they will find their caste and feel compatible knowing its rites and social mores, even though they cannot speak to its local members. Others claim that Hinduism provides a bond despite its diversity, that most Hindus know and revere certain gods, ceremonies, holy days, and sacred places.

Non-Hindus feel Indian, it is said, because India became a secular state and because they see that its great history includes many non-Hindu leaders and achievements. Indians living abroad share this Indianness, which is now based partly on a thriving popular culture, the promulgation of secular holidays, and the emergence of glamorous film, sport, and political personalities.[16]

Indians also express pride in the spread of their culture and note that they have had the greatest influence abroad through ideas, rather than through military or political coercion. Although Hinduism spread to Southeast Asia in the early Christian period, it does not diffuse easily, as it is based on the caste system and the associated belief in transmigration.

Buddhism, which originated in India, spread to East Asia, including China, and to Ceylon (now Sri Lanka) and Southeast Asia. Ironically, Buddhism almost disappeared in India while spreading abroad. Angkor Wat in Cambodia (now Kampuchea) and Borobadura in Indonesia remain as monuments to Indian cultural expansion in Southeast Asia, where Chinese and Indian ideas and influence have long competed.[17]

---

[15]Indians in the south feel their Indianness somewhat less intensely than those in the north. Southerners take pride in their own history and culture and in some ways feel superior to northerners, who had often been invaded by "barbarians." Bengalis are equally proud and independent. Regional and state loyalties remain strong, as pressure for the devolution of power from the central government to the states suggests.

[16]Nehru was proud of the vitality and success of Indians who went abroad, but worried about their mistreatment. He also recognized the limitation of what India could do for them in a foreign country. See Jawaharlal Nehru, *India's Foreign Policy,* Government of India, Ministry of Information and Broadcasting, New Delhi, 1983, p. 127.

[17]Indians sometimes refer to this area as "Greater India." Sinha and Ray, p. 4.

Indian political-military history does not provide the cohesive element that culture does. In the first place, the Indians did most of their fighting inside India, only rarely undertaking military ventures outside the subcontinent. They made a few incursions north into Afghanistan and Persia (now Iran), and these were often defensive (see Figure 3). They invaded Ceylon, but that island off the southern tip of India may be considered part of the region. In the south, they (notably the Cholas) made a few naval expeditions to Southeast Asia, but these brief adventures occurred nearly 1000 years ago.[18]

In only a few instances in Indian history were foreign incursions into India through the northwest passes stopped or defeated. Although a few Indian leaders appreciated the need for a forward strategy, such as the control of Afghanistan, they seldom had such strategies. As a result, Indian forces were compelled to fight on the defensive, on Indian soil, after the invaders had already gained access to the rich north Indian plain. In addition, the many Indian states seemed unable or unwilling to unite their forces against the invaders, thus enabling the aggressors to defeat the Indians piecemeal.

These military failures indicate that only infrequently did Indians give much thought or attach much importance to the strategic defense of India as a whole. The small states were concerned about themselves, not the larger entity. This point has not been lost on modern Indian leaders.

Indian campaigns against the assaults from the north also reveal that the Indian military technology through the ages lagged badly. For example, the Central Asians invented the saddle and stirrup and later used horse-mounted archers and developed tactics and maneuvers for their employment. Little evidence exists that the Indians ever adopted these improvements.[19] Until the British period, Indian armies clung to largely static warfare based on a corps of elephants, with some cavalry and masses of infantry.

Only the Chola kingdom and a few southern states appear to have maintained significant oceangoing navies.[20] The great Indian states

---

[18]The Chola king Rajendra's expeditions to Southeast Asia were "unique in the annals of India," according to A. L. Basham, *The Wonder That Was India,* Sidgwick & Jackson, London, 1967, p. 75. Kar (p. 110) states that Rajendra's "naval expeditions form a glorious chapter of our own maritime history. No Indian monarch before and after him even attained such conspicuous success in this field."

[19]The Guptas briefly experimented with some innovations but soon returned to their conservative and familiar forms of war.

[20]See footnote 18, above.

14

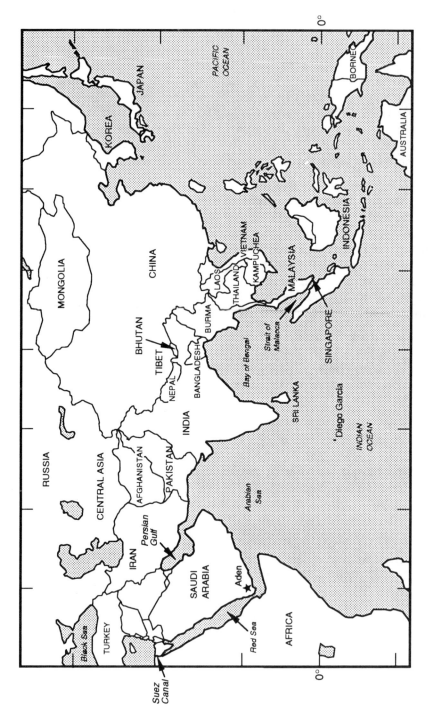

Figure 3—India Between Southeast and Southwest Asia

in the north had little interest in navies. The Moghuls' disastrous failure to perceive the need for a navy enabled Europeans to land unopposed on Indian shores.

Contemporary Indian naval planners have learned the lessons of India's severely limited naval tradition, and they are not unaware that most of India's trade was carried in foreign bottoms and protected by the Royal Navy during and briefly after the British raj. Although the Indians engaged in extensive international commercial activities, they themselves seldom sailed the ships.[21] After independence, according to one observer, "a new tradition had to be created."[22]

CULTURE

Contemporary Indian society is built on a great civilization that extends back more than 2500 years. Although the caste system and India's extensive linguistic and cultural diversity have changed over the centuries, the basic social and cultural patterns described by early Greek and Chinese travelers portray an India that is recognizable today.

Asked whether India will break up, as many countries are now doing, Indians usually answer that Indian culture is the binding force that will keep India united despite the strong regional subcultures and quarreling states that seem to threaten its existence. Many say also that democracy is a pillar of a unified India. Some add that the young and growing middle class is strengthening India and will support the Indian union.

The widely held perception that culture is a central feature of Indian life may be a greater force than the culture itself, which is slowly changing. Not surprisingly, Indian strategic thinking reflects and takes direction from this culture. The Brahmanic tradition, based on the ancient Indian epics, has a few generally accepted tenets and characteristics that seem to have influenced Indian strategic thinking, or the absence of it.

Hinduism, the basic element of Indian culture, is an amorphous body of beliefs resting on a few basic tenets. It has no "book," no accepted creed or god, no organized church, and no prophet. Ranging from the

---

[21]According to Thapar (p. 113), "Indians preferred to allow sailors of other nations to transport their goods."

[22]K. M. Pannikar, *Problems of Indian Defense*, Asia Publishing House, New York, 1960, p. 60.

lofty intellectual concepts of the Brahman to the very personal, emotional beliefs of the devotees of the gods Krishna and Shiva, and to the superstitions of the uneducated villagers, Hinduism is not a religion in the Western sense; it is more nearly a comprehensive way of life. It has adjusted to most invaders and penetrated the lives of Muslims, Christians, and Jews living in India.

The caste system, an integral and pervasive part of Brahmanic Hinduism and one that developed several centuries before Christ, has survived to this day. According to Brahman belief, the caste system is divinely ordained and hence unchangeable by man. The system probably originated in occupational classifications and evolved into its present form after the system of the four major classes, or *varna*, emerged about 500 BC.[23] The Brahmans were the teachers and priests, the Kshatriyas were the warrior-rulers, the Vaishyas were merchants and businessmen, and, at the bottom, the Shudra were workers and farmers. Outside the system were the non-Hindus, the so-called untouchables, now called Harijans (children of God).

Membership in one of the tens of thousands of castes, which are subdivisions of the classes, is based on birth and circumscribed by endogamy, the largest group within which a person may marry.[24] Some castes are found throughout India, while others are local. Although new castes may be formed and castes may move up and down the social ladder, the caste system has been much criticized because of its hierarchical nature and denial of individual liberties.[25] It has, nevertheless, been the bedrock of an amazingly stable society and a rich and lasting culture.

Caste and family have built up powerful loyalties that may compete with national allegiance. Moreover, the caste system has given Indians a hierarchical view not only of India but of the world; they rank nations by size, culture, and power. The caste system also suggests a stability and immutability in society and tends to foster a conservative and noninnovative mind-set—characteristics that describe many military establishments. However, this situation is changing, and wealth and education increasingly are slowly replacing caste as a measure of social status, especially in urban areas.

---

[23]The idea of *varna* may have influenced Plato's philosophical ordering in *The Republic*.

[24]The Sanskrit word for castes is *jati;* "caste" is of Portuguese origin (*casta*), meaning tribe, clan, or family. For the classic introduction to Indian civilization, see Basham, p. 149.

[25]It is much more difficult for an individual to move, as his caste is essential to his identity and place in society.

Dharma, karma, and transmigration are other powerful, generally accepted concepts of Hinduism. Dharma is natural law or social order or duty that is incumbent on every member of a caste. Karma describes an individual's actions and efforts within his caste, the results of which will determine his future incarnation through transmigration. How one acts in this life is thought to determine how one will improve or worsen in one's next. Many Indians say that their guidance for life comes from the *Gita,* which emphasizes the importance of an individual's performing his duty (dharma) and leading a moral life.[26]

To Indians, life is much more complex and less optimistic than in prevailing Western thought. They accept logic as one influence on life, but only one. Other influences include emotion, tradition, intuition, and fate. Accordingly, life is unknowable, but man must strive to follow his dharma. Fate is something to be dealt with, but also to be accepted.

The Indian view may be seen as a realistic and pragmatic approach to life, but it also can lead to a passive, almost fatalistic, acceptance of life. Many argue, however, that dharma requires that an individual strive to fulfill his moral obligations. Although most Indians deny that they are fatalists, the acceptance of life as it comes carries considerable weight among believers.

This complex view of life makes the future appear uncertain and less subject to human manipulation than it does to a Westerner. Rational analysis, so vital to Western societies, has less influence in Indian society, as so many other factors play important or dominant roles.[27] The acceptance of life as a mystery and the inability to manipulate events impedes preparation for the future in all areas of life, including the strategic.

The Indian belief in life cycles and repetitions, in particular, limits planning in the Western sense. To Indians, cycles constitute the basis of life and stand in stark contrast to the Western linear view of

---

[26]The *Bhagavad Gita* (Song of the Blessed One [Krishna]). Although many Indians take seriously the duty to lead a moral life, some in the lower castes accept their fate, as they see little chance of changing it. Although today many Indians no longer think specifically of transmigration, the tenet lingers in their psyche.

[27]One Indian told me that Indians had relied on intuition and emotion for a million years, so why should they give them up for logic, which is only a few thousand years old.

18

time.[28] An Indian is said to pass through four phases in life: student, homemaker, near hermit, and wanderer forsaking family and society until death. According to his actions (karma), he is reincarnated in another form, depending on the status he has earned, and begins the cycle over again.

Similarly, in the Indian view, the cosmos also goes through repeated cycles of creation, decay, destruction, and recreation. Unlike human cycles, cosmic cycles take millions or billions of years. Indian history also appears as a cycle of unity, decay, disunity, and reunification. A cyclical view suggests no past and no future, just a continuing series of cycles.[29]

The inherent pessimism and passivism of the cyclical view suggests little likelihood of major improvement in life, though dharma demands that one strive to lead a moral life. Even doing good deeds and leading the good life do not end the cycle. Only through renunciation of all desires, many Indians believe, can one break the cycle and join the Infinite in final peace and unity. That is, each individual has atman, or inner truth, which is one and the same as Brahma, the world spirit, the universal truth. Atman never ends; once free of the body, it soars and rejoins Brahma.

Thus, prevailing Indian beliefs, although changing in many ways, differ fundamentally from the Western views, which assume a faith in logic and human progress, the efficacy of individual efforts, a sense of history and continuity, and a future to be shaped and worked for. The more educated Indians, however, especially those versed in technology and economics, are coming to recognize the need for planning and an integrated conception of social and economic development. These tensions find expression in many contemporary policy dilemmas, including those associated with strategic concerns.

---

[28]de Riencourt (pp. 45, 102–105) argues that Indians have a spatial rather than a temporal view of life and reality and that this leads to the related conclusion that time does not exist.

[29]de Riencourt (p. 45) writes: "Since the process of time has no meaning, since history has no goal, every individual is merely reacting the same endless part, creating nothing new, making no original contribution to human progress." de Riencourt is wrong, of course, as Indians over the years have made great contributions to human knowledge and understanding, including the concept of zero and the nine so-called Arabic numerals, which the Arabs introduced to the West in the ninth century.

THE BRITISH RAJ

The British East India Company used the Moghul's imperial administrative structure for its own purposes as it spread over India. Following the Indian mutiny of 1857, the British government took over from the company, and Queen Victoria supplanted the Moghul emperor. Using the Moghul structure as a starting point, the British began to mold India into a single administrative entity.

The British brought modern technology, railroads, and the telegraph, thereby improving transportation and providing modern nationwide communications, important parts of the necessary infrastructure of a modern state. They introduced English as a common language for education and government and organized a more modern educational system, open to a wider range of Indians, than was available under the Moghuls. The British also instituted a single legal system with courts for all. The Indian civil service, though predominantly British until the 1940s, was one of the world's best civil bureaucracies, and many of its skills were ultimatey transferred to India.

All of these measures contributed to the development of a modern Indian nation-state with a unified administration, individual rights, and representative government in the form of a parliamentary system. Some have argued that administrative unity produces the state, then nationalism develops.[30] India, however, was simultaneously exposed to and influenced by the powerful nationalism at work at the time in Europe. As one scholar observed:

> European history glorified the nineteenth century flowering of nationalism as a spiritual renewal and political endeavor and posited the nation state as the highest and natural form of politics.[31]

British nationalism and pride, which the Indians easily sensed from their contacts with the British, especially aroused Indian nationalism.

Thus, British efforts to develop a unified colony laid the foundations for Indian unity, and the British concept of nationalism nurtured

[30]See Ainslie T. Embree, *India's Search for National Identity,* Chanakya Publications, New Delhi, 1987, p. 2.

[31]Judith M. Brown, *Modern India: The Origins of an Asian Democracy,* Oxford University Press, New Delhi, 1988, p. 147.

Indian nationalism. Indians realized, however, that the English applied their ideas of democracy and equality to themselves, but not to Indians. Because of this racism, the English became the focus of nationalist resentment, thus adding a third powerful factor to the developing Indian nationalism.[32]

More important for this study, the British began to consider the strategic defense of a unified India.[33] Because they had arrived by sea, the British perceived the need to protect India from future naval attacks, especially from their European rivals. Accordingly, they evolved an Indian maritime strategy subsumed under a British global strategy to gain and maintain supremacy of all the oceans and to control the world's major choke points, especially those leading to the Indian Ocean.

The British gained control of the Suez Canal and established a base at Aden, which together gave them control of the most direct route from Europe, the most likely source of naval threat to India (see Figure 2, above). In addition, the British gained suzerainty over Malaya and established Singapore in the early nineteenth century. This gave them control of the Strait of Malacca, the most important passage into the Indian Ocean from the Far East (see Figure 3, above). The British also dominated the waters off the Cape of Good Hope in southern Africa, thus denying to hostile powers the use of the original European route to India.[34] British domination of the high seas turned the Indian Ocean into a British lake.

The British did not develop an Indian navy.[35] In World War II, a small Indian naval force served with the Royal Navy, but it lacked the necessary support elements to rank as an independent navy. Indian officers, being junior, gained only limited experience. The Indians inherited a small navy at independence but paid little attention to it.

---

[32]Some Indians have said that India would still be part of the British empire had it not been for British racism. According to others (for example, Chaudhuri, p. 31), nationalism developed as a negative movement against the British, and the lack of any positive goals greatly weakened it.

[33]As noted above, Indians had been aware of invasions and threats, especially from the northwest, for centuries but had made few, if any, attempts at a unified or explicit strategy. The states sought only to defend their own limited areas.

[34]Given the disorganized expansion of the British empire in Asia, not all of these acquisitions were originally seen as part of India's defense, but all became incorporated in it. Although unable to control the straits in the Dutch East Indies empire, the British gained footholds in North Borneo and developed northern Australia to counter the Dutch.

[35]See Pannikar, p. 59. A very small Indian navy was created in 1924, but it was unable to defend even local waters.

As British naval power declined after World War II and withdrew from east of Suez in 1967, Indians realized the extent of their dependence on the British and began to organize their own navy. The lack of a naval tradition, the possession of only a few old Royal Navy vessels, and the general lack of an interest in naval matters meant that the Indians had to start almost from scratch in the 1960s.

The land defense of India presented a more familiar but still difficult problem. While the mountains served as barriers in most places, several passes in the northwest had served for centuries as the main invasion routes. The rugged terrain and independent tribesmen found in these areas added to the difficulties. Furthermore, in the nineteenth century Russia was expanding into Central Asia and looking southward, and the British began to view Russia as the primary land threat in the northwest.

However, neither Russia nor a weakened China threatened India from the northern and northeastern frontiers. Nevertheless, by the middle of the nineteenth century, the British had taken Burma, which they governed from India, as a defense against China. Although China also claimed Tibet, the British kept it in their sphere of influence.

In the northwest, the British tried to develop a layered defense, using diplomatic as well as military means. They first sought to establish a buffer system as far out from India as possible. This meant keeping Afghanistan and Iran friendly and out of the Russian sphere of influence. It also meant keeping Tibet out of Chinese and Russian control in the north. The second layer of the plan called for employing the northwest tribesmen as a defense screening force. The British, as the Moghuls had before them, gained the tribesmen's support with subsidies. Neither layer of the strategy worked perfectly, as the Afghan wars and the constant skirmishes among or with the tribesmen attest.

Finally, the British planned for the defense of India itself if these other efforts failed. This eventuality materialized only in World War II. The British vacillated between a policy of forward employment of some army troops in the buffer areas and keeping them back in India for the direct defense of India.

The British empire at the end of the nineteenth century and the first half of the twentieth had become a status quo power. Its main purpose was to protect what it had. Consequently, British strategy was defensive in general, and particularly so for India. The 1907 Russo-British Agreement divided Iran into spheres of influence and reduced the problems of the northwest considerably. Unfortunately, the tribesmen were generally at war or ignored the agreement, and to this day unruly groups continue to operate in Pakistan. By World War I, the British had recognized Chinese suzerainty over Tibet but still advocated its independence.

London decided imperial policy and goals, but Indian security strategy was formulated largely in India and was developed from an Indian perspective. The British formed the large, all-volunteer Indian Army with a large contingent of British troops and British officers. This force was organized to protect Britain's most important colony and also to provide for internal security. It also helped to protect other parts of the British empire and fought in both world wars.

India inherited about two-thirds of the Indian Army, minus the British troops and officers, at independence. The Indian Army, at the request of the new civil leaders, played a role in persuading reluctant leaders in Hyderabad and Kashmir to join in the formation of the Indian union. It fought to defend Kashmir from tribal and Pakistani attack in 1947–1948. The Indian government has subsequently called on the Army to quell intermittent internal disturbances. It has acted as a strong factor for Indian unity.

After World War II, the world around India changed. India and Pakistan became independent, China grew more powerful than it had been, and England began to lose interest. The defensive apparatus of an empire that had protected India so well in the past no longer existed for India. The gradual reduction of the British Navy opened India's seaward front. On land, Pakistan, now independent, began to challenge India, starting in 1947 in Kashmir. A strong and ambitious communist government took over China in 1949 after a long civil war, and soon seemed to confront India on its borders.

At the time of independence, India possessed very limited resources for defense and no experience in strategic planning. It inherited much from the British raj, but it had to develop its own strategy and means of defense for the second half of the twentieth century. Neither effort has been completed, but strategic ideas are emerging, and considerable effort and progress has been made in creating military forces.

2. INDIAN SECURITY STRATEGY: THE VIEW FROM DELHI

This section examines India's security strategy in a way favored by many Indians: as a series of circles or rings (mandala).[1] The first circle is India itself. The second circle encompasses India's smaller contiguous neighbors: Sri Lanka, Nepal, Bangladesh, and the Maldives (see Figure 1, Section 1, above).

The third circle includes Pakistan, the only subcontinental state that has dared to challenge Indian regional military power; China, India's giant Asian rival; and the Soviet Union, India's best friend and partner in the geopolitical sphere of Asia, and perhaps the world. The Indian Ocean region as a whole forms a fourth ring, which Indians believe contains both opportunities and threats (see Figure 3, Section 1, above). The final circle includes the more distant great powers and the rest of the world.

Delhi's strategic community places the entire subcontinent in the first circle, believing that it constitutes a single strategic unit defined by geography and culture.[2] Pakistan, Nepal, Bhutan, Bangladesh, and Sri Lanka are seen as basically of Indian culture, though differences have obviously existed in the past and more have developed since their independence.

The British evolved the concept of the subcontinent as a strategic unit out of imperial necessity, and they went to great lengths to protect this most valuable part of their empire. But they did not share the fundamental belief, deeply embedded in the Indian psyche, that the unity of the subcontinent reflects the integrity and dreams of a people and constitutes an integral part of their social fabric.

The strategy of defending the subcontinental land border may seem like an offensive strategy, given the subcontinent's political makeup today. But Indians regard the strategy as purely defensive, just as

---

[1]The Indian government has never articulated its security strategy in any one place or time. The mandala concept is based on Kautilya's mandala, but applied more broadly here. According to the concept, a nation's contiguous neighbors are always seen as enemies and their outer neighbors as friends, etc., in a series of circles. See *Kautilya's Arthashastra,* translated by Dr. R. Shamasastry, Mysore Printing and Publishing House, Mysore, 1967, pp. 22–24. Kautilya, a Brahman adviser to the Mauryans, used the mandala concept in describing his work on the art of government.

[2]The northern part, at least, of the Indian Ocean is included in this definition.

having the navy keep hostile powers far from India's shores is seen as defensive. Given the political configuration of South Asia today, this image of the unity of the subcontinent raises two separate but closely related security problems for India:

- The internal unity of India itself
- The security of India and its small, contiguous neighbors, now politically independent, but in Indian eyes still an integral part of India's strategic defense.

Indians do not readily admit publicly that they hold this concept of the strategic unity of the subcontinent. However, to understand India's security actions and policies relating to its close neighbors and Indians' extreme sensitivities about other nations' intruding or trying to gain influence in this region, the observer must recognize that Indians do indeed regard security in terms of the strategic unity of the subcontinent.

INDIA: THE REGIONAL CORE

India's most pressing strategic security concern is its own internal unity. In looking back on their country's history, Indian nationalists, though highlighting the periods of unity and splendor, have expressed concern about the much longer periods of conflict and disunity. Today, they are confronted by the same ethnic, linguistic, regional, and communal factors, one or more of which have torn India asunder after each brief period of unity.

The nationalists have also noted the numerous successful invasions of India, mostly through the northwest passes, now controlled by a hostile Pakistan. In the past, India failed to defeat most of these invaders because of both internal disunity and technological backwardness. Indians thus see a close relationship between internal security and outside aggression. They know that without internal unity, external defense will remain difficult and hazardous.

Kashmir illustrates the conjunction of the dual threats stemming from weak internal security and outside aggression: The Kashmiris are revolting inside India, and the Pakistanis are supporting them from the outside. It explains why much of Delhi's strategic community refuses to compromise on this issue. To do so would be a major and potentially catastrophic compromise of India's most vital interest—its own internal security and unity as well as its belief in a secular state.

To better understand India's obsession with internal unity and integrity, it is useful to look again at its history. All periods of unity were based on empires assembled and held together by force. These emerged from smaller Indian states, or they were formed by foreign invaders who settled in India and became Indian. The last two empires, however, were built by foreigners: the Moghuls and the British, who assimilated to a lesser degree than earlier outsiders, the former accommodating with the Hindus, the latter hardly at all.

The Moghul and British empires, also put together by force, were never real unions, but collections of states, many with long histories, their own language and culture, and a tradition of independence. The smaller states disliked being ruled by either Indian or foreign emperors and constantly revolted. They were in the process of overthrowing the Moghul empire when the British arrived.

The various emperors seldom succeeded in developing strong imperial or Indian loyalties, much less in integrating the various states they had conquered into a union. Even the British ruled only a portion of India directly. The so-called princely states retained their own rulers and not insignificant powers of self-rule until independence. Each ruler was concerned with his own state and distrusted the other states; none cared about Indian unity.

On arriving in India, the British observed that the idea of empire was fairly popular, and they quietly worked under the Moghul imperial umbrella. After Indian soldiers—both Hindu and Muslim—revolted against the British in 1857, often called the great mutiny by the British and the first war of independence by the Indians, the British abolished the Moghul empire and made it a part of the British empire; thus, India became an empire within an empire. While the ruling elite changed from Moghul to British, much continued as before.

The British expanded the Moghul empire and continued their centralizing efforts. As noted in Section 1, they provided efficient administration, a common law and language, and the modern technology, railroads, and telegraph that pulled the empire together. Many Indians give the British credit for creating modern India even as they criticize the British for retarding the growth of the Indian state, plundering India economically, and delaying independence.

The British treated India as a separate empire. For example, London gave the British rulers in India considerable autonomy, allowing them to look at the strategic defense of India from an Indian perspective. London, of course, continued to view defense from the perspective of the larger British empire.

The Indian nationalists of the late nineteenth and early twentieth centuries led the independence movement and adopted the European ideas of nationalism and the nation-state. They were too few in number to win independence by themselves, but Gandhi rallied the masses around these ideas, though they may not have fully understood them.

Although the new nationalism propelled India toward independence, it has not supplanted regional traditions and loyalties. Within India, the various states retain their identities and subcultures, and several would, if independent, rank among the largest states in the world. Uttar Pradesh, for example, has over 150 million people, and Andhra Pradesh, in the south, over 60 million.

Many leading Indian strategists recall that their grandparents had identified themselves by caste, locality, and language rather than as Indians or Hindus, thus suggesting that at independence the new nationalism had by no means replaced the old loyalties. On the eve of independence, India remained a collection of states with a broad common culture but many subcultures, differing from each other in language and tradition, and held together politically by strong British rule.

When India became independent on August 16, 1947, nationalist euphoria ran high, but beneath the surface not a great deal had changed. Most princely states opted to join India; several preferred to remain independent, but were not allowed to. The fissiparous forces that Nehru had strongly warned against were very much alive, and the new Indian unity was a fragile one.

The new Indian ruling elite, many of whom were Brahmans, tended to rule from Delhi as masters, somewhat like the British. Their first challenge was the integration of the Indian princely states into a new republic.[3] This required the use of force, and of the new Indian Army, on several occasions. The task was accomplished largely by Sardar Patel, Nehru's conservative and practical alter ego, and the Indian Army. Nehru's consuming involvement in international affairs and world statesmanship led him to pay less attention to the internal problems that he had earlier written about so eloquently, though he pushed hard for Indian unity and economic development necessary for a free country.

---

[3]The Indian constitution approved in 1950 provides for a federal system that takes into account the divisions within India while trying to mold a union. In recent years, the central government has taken on more and more power, and the states have now begun to call for the devolution of authority to the local level.

Since 1947, successive Indian governments have relied on a mix of force and inducement to deal with problems of integration and unity. The various police and paramilitary forces that were raised to suppress separatist movements throughout the country and to maintain order now approach the regular armed forces in size. The Indian constitution also permits the central government to take over state governments and rule them by presidential decree from Delhi. An emergency was declared from 1975 to 1977 over all of India, and civil rights and freedoms have at other times been curtailed in many regions of the country.

The central government has also frequently called on the Army to maintain order and to suppress insurgencies and revolts. In several cases (such as those involving the Nagas and the Mizos in northeast India) military pressure was followed by economic and political inducements, and many separatist groups have laid down their arms. Yet these are tactics, or perhaps a strategy for dealing with internal revolts, but they are not a strategy of national integration.

Some Indian strategists argue that these periods of separatist, ethnic, and communal unrest are cyclical and simply part of the Indian way of life. Others see gradual progress and are more optimistic about the future. Thus far, however, few efforts have led to a long-term, constructive strategy entailing mass literacy programs, national educational standards, linguistic unification, and other measures of national integration. The apparent neglect of national integration efforts contrasts sharply with specific actions undertaken by other ethnically diverse Asian societies, such as Indonesia.[4]

THE SMALL NEIGHBORS: POINTS OF VULNERABILITY

None of its smaller neighbors—except perhaps Pakistan—poses a serious military threat to India.[5] However, India sees these neighbors as threatening in other ways.

- First, with the exception of Sri Lanka, India's neighbors have been ruled predominantly by nondemocratic governments.

Until recently Pakistan and Bangladesh were ruled by the military; Nepal and Bhutan are kingdoms; and all four are seen as inherently

---

[4]Indonesia has adopted and educated its people in one national language, promulgated five principles of national ideology, *Pancasila,* and through socioeconomic measures tried to demonstrate the opportunities and value of Indonesian unity.

[5]Pakistan is discussed in the subsection immediately following.

unstable. Indians believe that most South Asian peoples, as opposed to governments, share their view of the cultural unity of the region and its common security problems. If these states had democratic regimes, Indians argue, accommodationist views would surface and support Indian positions on regional security and integrity; in other words, stabler governments would collaborate more actively with India. This view is now being put to the test as Pakistan, Bangladesh, and Nepal all have fledgling democracies. Pakistan, however, remains a special case.

- Second, these states have ethnic and communal problems similar to those of India, and some of these problems spill over present political boundaries, creating security problems for India.

Examples include Kashmiris in India and Pakistan; Tamils in Sri Lanka and Tamil Nadu (southern India); Bengalis in Bangladesh, West Bengal, and western India; and tribal problems in northeast India, often involving Burma and China. The increase in national consciousness has made ethnic movements a threat to the integrity of all nations in the region, as politicians often use ethnic groups in all the states to further their own particular goals. Ethnic problems seem to be increasing, and they are likely to continue to create difficulties for India, as well as other governments of the region.

- Third, these small states have often sought support and aid from powers outside the immediate region so as to balance India's preponderance of power.

While the smaller states see the search for balance as a natural and almost necessary step, Delhi considers it a betrayal of regional integrity. Sri Lanka's flirtation with the United States and others, as well as Nepal's and Bangladesh's opening to China, have created anxiety in India that has led India to try to counteract all such activities. Indeed, Kautilya long ago warned against the intrigue of foreign kings "as a threat to one's own security," even as he accepted intrigue and the use of internal spies as legitimate self-defense measures.[6]

- Fourth, Indians suffer from a pervasive fear of the "foreign hand" at work among India's unstable neighbors and in India.

---

[6]Kautilya, often referred to as Chanakya, preceded Machiavelli in a cynical and amoral approach to strategy. See *Kautilya's Arthashastra*, pp. 22–24.

Although the Indians seldom name these foreigners, they are perceived to be the Chinese, sponsors of revolutionary wars and tribal unrest; the Americans in the form of the ubiquitous CIA; and the Pakistanis.[7] On the one hand, foreigners undoubtedly have at times intrigued and interfered in India's domestic affairs and those of its neighbors. On the other hand, the Indians sometimes blame the foreigners to such an extent that they overlook the inherent instability of some of their region and of their neighbors.

Indians also fail to understand, or they reluctantly accept, a neighbor's need to use foreigners to offset India's dominating influence, as they do not see themselves as a threat to their neighbors. Moreover, India has engaged in similar disruptive practices. In 1971, it interfered in East Pakistan and more recently in Sri Lanka. India's Research and Analysis Wing (RAW), its principal intelligence agency, is widely believed to have been involved in both cases.

Indians see these actions as less reprehensible than similar actions by neighbors against them, as Indians believe that their security (1) must take priority in the region and (2) generally benefits all of South Asia. Thus, India's regional strategy suggests two core perceptions:

- India will not allow a neighboring state to undertake any action in foreign affairs or defense policy that India deems potentially inimical to Indian security.

- India will not permit foreign governments to establish a presence or influence in a neighboring state that India views as unfriendly.

Some have described this as the "Indira Doctrine," and it is not unlike the Monroe Doctrine. Indians believe, however, that their approach is firmly based on the cultural and geographical unity of the subcontinent. The Monroe Doctrine, in contrast, covered a vast area with no geographical unity and included countries with somewhat different cultures, languages, and histories.

To advance this regional strategy, India built on earlier British treaties and agreements that restricted the freedom of its neighbors in their foreign and defense policies. Under treaties with Nepal and Bhutan, neither can take security actions of which India does not approve. The strategic location of Nepal and Bhutan atop the Himalayas constitutes a critical element in Indian defense against possible Chinese threats.

---

[7]Even after considerable improvement in Indo-American relations, some Indians still blamed the CIA for Prime Minister Rajiv Gandhi's assassination in May 1991.

The 1972 Treaty of Friendship with Bangladesh, though less specific on security matters than the Himalayan nation treaties, sought to prevent Bangladesh from initiating unfriendly security policies. Similarly, a letter attachment to the 1987 accords between India and Sri Lanka limited the latter's freedom of action with respect to foreign use of the harbor of Trincomalee, its employment of security advisers from abroad, and the establishment of foreign broadcasting facilities on its territory.

Delhi has also applied political and economic pressure to change the policies of its smaller neighbors. In the mid-1970s, India supported groups in Sikkim that favored union with India. When in the late 1980s Nepal and India disagreed over the renewal of their treaties covering trade and transit, India applied strong economic pressure to landlocked Nepal. The crisis was settled in 1990, after India yielded to Nepal on several key points; since then, however, internal changes in Nepal have brought to power a more pro-Indian government.[8]

India has intervened militarily in its smaller neighbors' affairs when it felt threatened by their internal discord. In 1970–1971, Prime Minister Indira Gandhi regarded the disturbances in East Pakistan as potentially threatening to all of eastern India, as masses of refugees were pouring over the border. The disturbances gave her the opportunity to cut Pakistan in two, an intervention that led to the partition of Pakistan and the creation of an initially friendly Bangladesh.

Again in 1987, Indira Gandhi's son and successor, Rajiv Gandhi, intervened in Sri Lanka to protect the Tamil minority, to ensure the integrity of Sri Lanka, and to help bring about a peaceful settlement of the Tamil insurgency on the island.[9] According to a Calcutta editor, "thanks to him [Rajiv Gandhi], Pakistan is South Asia's only other truly independent nation."[10]

The Maldive government in 1988 called on India for help during a coup attempt; India responded immediately, then promptly withdrew

---

[8]In May 1991, the Nepali Congress, backed by the Indian Congress, won the national election to form a new democratic government. However, the opposition in 1992 is threatening the pro-Indian government.

[9]The Indian Army intervened ostensibly to protect the Tamils and ensure their welfare and to preserve the integrity of Sri Lanka. After the arrival of the Indian Peacekeeping Force (IPKF), the Tamil Tigers, the most militant Tamil group, refused to accommodate, and the IPKF in effect began to fight the Tamil Tigers, but the Tigers and the Sri Lankan government remained far apart.

[10]Sunanda K. Datta-Ray, editor of the *Statesman* (Calcutta), "India's Monroe Doctrine," *The Sunday Statesman,* August 2, 1987, p. 1.

its troops after the crisis ended.[11] Even though many in the Indian
Army in retrospect viewed the Sri Lankan intervention as a mistake,
Indian hawks strongly defend the operation and assert that they
would advocate similar operations in the future when important
Indian interests are at stake.

These Indian interventions seem to conflict with the declared policy of
Nehru and his successors that Delhi recognizes its neighbors'
sovereignty, territorial integrity, and autonomy in their domestic
matters. But the policy does not apply when matters of India's national interest are involved.[12] This may seem like a contradiction to
Westerners, but it does not to Indians. The situation decides the policy, and India's interests will always dominate in such circumstances.
Where the subcontinent is concerned, pragmatism and self-interest
prevail over morality and idealism.

The tension between India and its neighbors stems from (1) different
concepts of regional security and (2) India's size. For Indians, the
subcontinent's cultural and geographical unity implies a strategic
unity, even if the region remains divided into various states. The
subcontinent's smaller nations, in contrast, emphasize their political
independence and seek to establish an identity of their own.

This tension is reflected in the South Asian Association for Regional
Cooperation (SAARC). Delhi fears that its neighbors will use SAARC
to gang up on India, while its neighbors fear that large and powerful
India will use SAARC as a forum to control them. India has always
insisted on bilateral relations with these nations; but for them, fear
and suspicion of India lurks just beneath the surface. Their concern
should not be surprising, given India's disproportionate power and its
willingness to intervene when it perceives threats to its own interests.

PAKISTAN: THE REGIONAL DESTABILIZER

Most Indian strategists consider Pakistan a unique case, threatening
vital Indian interests in multiple ways:

- Pakistan's existence breaches the unity of the subcontinent and
  thus threatens its security.

---

[11]The Maldives purportedly turned first to Sri Lanka, the United States, and
possibly Singapore for assistance, all of which declined. However, American naval assets helped India track down and capture the fleeing mercenaries.

[12]A few Indians contend that there are no fully sovereign states around India except Pakistan. Others disagree. The various treaties and restrictions on its neighbors
suggest the contention has some basis.

- Geostrategically, Pakistan, a hostile power, sits astride the main land invasion routes into India.

- Pakistan's armed forces have remained a threat and have imposed a heavy defense burden on India, but they do not challenge India's survival.

- Pakistan's military power draws Indian power away from the defense of the subcontinent as a whole.

- Pakistan has developed a navy that could interfere with Indian access to Middle East oil and other Indian interests in that region.

- Pakistan has brought hostile outside powers into the subcontinent through its alliances; at various times these have included the United States, China, and several Islamic states.

- Since 1947, Pakistan has aided and abetted separatists and other destabilizing movements inside India, for example, in the Punjab and Kashmir.[13]

- Finally, Pakistan's Islamic professions threaten Indian secularism; its ties to other Islamic nations are a source of financial and other support; and the specter of Islamic fundamentalism surrounding India, in the view of Indians, amounts to encirclement by hostile elements. Pakistan even talks of an "Islamic [nuclear] bomb."

Indian politicians viewed the 1947 partition and creation of Pakistan as an unfortunate but temporary breach in the strategic unity of the subcontinent.[14] Kashmir also quickly became a bone of contention. The accession to India of the Hindu Maharaja of Kashmir with strong Indian support or pressure angered the Pakistanis, who viewed Kashmir as a Muslim state that should have belonged to Pakistan. The accession agreement provided for a popular vote on the issue, but the vote never took place.

Even before the Maharaja of Kashmir opted to join India, tribal elements, aided and abetted by Pakistan, had infiltrated that state; they were later joined by Pakistani army units. The fighting continued until January 1, 1949, when a cease-fire was drawn across the middle of Kashmir. Thus, from its inception, smaller Pakistan took the initiative and challenged India, its unity, and its assumption of primacy

---

[13]These low-level conflicts have repeatedly inflamed Indo-Pakistani relations, as they threaten India's vital concern for its unity. Furthermore, Pakistan's tactics are difficult to counter; they represent a low-cost option for Pakistan, but an expensive response for India.

[14]Most Indians now accept Pakistan as permanent.

in the region. Pakistan has generally kept India on the strategic defensive ever since.

Although Kashmir has been a continuing and visible source of serious conflict between the two countries, Indians regard Pakistan's refusal to accept the primacy of India in the region as the basic issue of contention between the two countries. Pakistan, about one-eighth the size of India, had been a part of Indian history for hundreds of years, and though it is Muslim, most Indians believe that it shares the same culture.[15]

Adding the threat of injury to insult, Pakistan has developed a military capability out of proportion to its size. It has gained the support of two great powers—the United States and China—and secured financial assistance from fellow Muslims in the Middle East. Few Indian strategists believe that Pakistan can destroy their country, but through propaganda, infiltration, and subversion, and especially its encouragement of secessionist movements, Islamabad can create serious difficulties for Delhi.

India was America's first choice as a regional anticommunist ally, and Indian leaders hinted that the United States and India could forge a strategic partnership. For the American leadership of the 1940s and 1950s, however, Pakistan, though less attractive, was a more eager partner, as India preferred its policy of nonalignment.

Pakistan thus became a member of the two anticommunist treaty groups formed to contain the Soviets and the Chinese in Asia: the Central Treaty Organization (CENTO) and the South-East Asia Treaty Organization (SEATO). By 1958, American military aid had provided Pakistan with the foundation of a modern army, a development that further alienated the Indians. This led Delhi to explore the possibilities of closer relations with the Soviet Union.

Delhi did not initially respond to the rearmament of Pakistan with a substantial buildup of its own. Nehru, determined to keep defense spending under control, counted on the United States to restrain Pakistan. Only after the Sino-Indian conflict of 1962 did India feel compelled to expand its military forces—with American, British, and Soviet help. The Indian buildup, in turn, frightened Pakistan, which launched probing attacks in the Rann of Kutch in April 1965 and larger attacks on Indian Kashmir in September. The Pakistani ini-

---

[15]The two nations do in many ways have the same culture, as most Muslims are converted Indians who eat the same food (eschewing pork), enjoy the same music, and share a long history.

tiative in Kashmir failed, and the Soviet Union, trying its hand as regional peacemaker, arranged a cease-fire. The Tashkent agreement of January 1966 ended the war.

Pakistan then took other steps to improve its military position. It began to look to the Islamic Middle East for support and financial backing; it also received substantial military assistance from the People's Republic of China (PRC).

As India perceived the development of an "Islamabad-Washington-Peking axis," it actively cultivated the Soviet Union to counterbalance both the PRC and the United States.[16] After deciding to attack East Pakistan, Prime Minister Gandhi in August 1971 hastily signed the friendship treaty that India and the Soviet Union had been discussing since 1969. This move was deliberately calculated to neutralize the PRC when India became militarily involved in East Pakistan.

After Pakistan attacked India in the west (some believe that India provoked the attack), the Indian Army, in December 1971, quickly marched into East Pakistan and set up the government of Bangladesh. This initiative—the first against Pakistan—helped India regain its self-respect and status in the subcontinent after its 1962 defeat by China. However, the Indians deeply resented the dispatch of the USS Enterprise into the Bay of Bengal, a late and futile U.S. gesture to support Pakistan. The Simla agreement of 1972, which ended the war, stated that all Indo-Pakistani differences should be settled by peaceful means.

To the chagrin and surprise of the Indian strategic community, Pakistan recovered from the 1971 defeat, and began work on its "Islamic bomb." By the 1980s, Pakistan was receiving considerable military assistance from several states and was on its way to becoming a powerful military, and possibly nuclear, power.

Indians continue to take the Pakistani threat very seriously, and much of Delhi's diplomacy and strategic maneuvering is devoted to balancing and countering Islamabad. In the region, India strongly opposes Pakistan's efforts to provide military assistance to India's regional neighbors, especially Sri Lanka, as India sees such aid as another effort to weaken it and challenge it in the region.

India's entire Afghanistan policy flows from the principle of "my enemy's enemy is my friend," and Indian strategists often quoted

---

[16]India's friendship with the Soviet Union was a major break with the British policy of opposing Russia and denying it a meaningful role on the subcontinent.

Kautilya to justify their steady support of whatever regime rules in Kabul, as long as that regime is hostile to Pakistan. India has tried to contest Pakistan's natural advantage in the Islamic world with the claim that it has more Muslims than Pakistan; it even declares that this large Muslim population makes it an "Islamic" state.[17] This tactic backfired at the 1969 Rabat meeting of the Organization of the Islamic Conference, which refused India membership. India has also tried to counter Pakistan's efforts in the Middle East Islamic countries.[18]

Indian strategists remain perplexed and concerned about Pakistan. Activists argue that India should take such actions as the 1971 attack on East Pakistan more often and wrest the initiative from Pakistan. General Sundarji's bold 1987 *Brass Tacks* exercise on the Pakistani border, while he was chief of the Army Staff, was somewhat controversial, but no similar exercises have followed.

In sum, India has devised no overall strategy to deal with Pakistan. The government finds itself in an expensive arms race with a much smaller country that has parlayed its relations with outside powers to great advantage. More recently, India has been alarmed by Pakistan's nuclear program, which threatens to reduce the strategic gap between the two. Pakistan is now believed to have nuclear weapons. Finally, Pakistan's alleged support of low-level terrorism and insurrection poses a threat to Indian domestic security.

These perceived Pakistani threats are particularly dangerous as they strike India's most sensitive nerve—its fragile national unity. As long as Pakistan continues to challenge India's primacy in the region and create trouble inside India, the relationship will not improve though both sides seem to realize that war is not the answer.[19]

CHINA: THE MAJOR RIVAL

Because of its size, population, and military might, including a nuclear capability, Indians consider China the major external military

---

[17]India also tried to develop close ties to the new Iranian revolutionary government and sent a Muslim delegation to Tehran. The Iranians were not cordial, perhaps remembering the willingness of India to become part of the shah's regional strategic system.

[18]India's relations with the Middle East are discussed below (this section) under the heading of "Beyond South Asia: The Indian Ocean Region."

[19]Talks at the secretary level are taking place in 1991–1992. The two sides have also agreed not to strike each other's nuclear installations. Tensions rise and fall, but calm heads have prevailed thus far, and they have not fought a war for over 20 years.

threat, though it has not proved as steadily and actively hostile to India as has Pakistan. In Indian eyes, however, China is at least a fitting and worthy opponent. Nehru wrote that, unlike some of India's smaller neighbors, India and China were the only states that embodied entire civilizations. The Chinese threat has three components:

- A direct challenge along the 4000-kilometer China-India border
- An indirect threat from Beijing's support of India's other neighbors, especially Pakistan
- A potential challenge to Indian preeminence in South Asia.

The two also compete in the Middle East and in Southeast Asia.

The Sino-Indian border war of 1962 was India's greatest humiliation since independence. Nehru had expected the two states to cooperate and had gone out of his way to bring China into the family of nations. China's takeover of Tibet in 1950 disturbed some Indian strategists, but Nehru accepted it in the 1954 Sino-Indian Agreement.

In the preamble to that treaty, India and China agreed on *Panchsheel* (five principles): respect for each other's territorial integrity and sovereignty, mutual nonaggression, mutual noninterference in each other's internal affairs, equality and mutual benefit, and peaceful coexistence. Nehru extended these five principles to relationships among all nations.

Border tensions and incidents nevertheless escalated, and the Chinese finally attacked India in 1962. The incursion shocked Nehru and, in view of some, may have contributed to his death. Ostensibly a Chinese reaction to what it saw as Indian intrusion into Chinese territory along the border, the attack's broader purpose seems to have been to humble India and expose its weakness, as well as to prove that the PRC was a major player in South Asia.

Border disputes have remained a problem, with serious tension recurring in 1987. Indian passions have since subsided, and Rajiv Gandhi visited China in 1988. Subsequent low-level talks, conducted by the secretariat-level Joint Working Group, have met with little enthusiasm on either side for a definitive solution.

The solution will take time to work out, as the approaches to the problem differ. India bases its arguments on what it sees as historical facts, while China seeks a political deal. After the 1962 war, the Indian government vowed not to give up any more Indian territory.

Moreover, public opinion would probably not allow the Indian government to give up any Indian territory at this time. More recently, Prime Ministers Rao and Li Peng agreed in December 1991 that the Joint Working Group should meet regularly and discuss specific solutions. The group met in February 1992 in Delhi.

India for several reasons sees China's close and continuing relationship with Pakistan as a serious threat. China has provided military, perhaps even including nuclear, aid. It might support Pakistan in times of crisis and, under certain scenarios, help with a second front against India. China's resentment of India's special relationship with the former Soviet Union exacerbated the situation, though improvements in Sino-Soviet relations in the 1980s diminished these concerns.

Because of the threat of a war with China and Pakistan, Indian strategists must plan for at least a two-front war. While interior lines confer certain advantages, the distances between the fronts are great and India's transportation system has a limited capacity for large-scale troop movement. One can only guess at India's strategic or operational plans for defeating a two-pronged threat.

India has most likely adopted a version of the famous Schlieffen Plan of World War I. India's position poses similar problems to those faced by Germany: a small, fast-mobilizing country on the west and a larger, but slower, country on the east. The plan would entail a quick defeat of Pakistan while the ten mountain divisions and the Indian Air Force held the Chinese in check. Once Pakistan was defeated, the main elements of the Indian Army would move to the eastern front for the longer, larger struggle against the Chinese.

Those concerned with the Indian Navy also fear Chinese naval expansion and increased activity in the Indian Ocean. Chinese submarines have been reported in the Indian Ocean, and several Chinese naval vessels have visited Bangladesh and Pakistan. However, given China's ancient submarines and limited surface fleet, the threat is not considered serious at this time. China's naval capabilities may be more a rationalization for India's naval development than an immediate and serious threat to its vital security objectives.

The border dispute in northernmost India (see Figure 1, above) is the most obvious issue between the two powers, but the basic problem is the role and place of each in the region. India had hoped to play the leading role in South Asia, but China, with its 1962 intrusion, has indicated that it too wants an important place. India and China have competed for the most part peacefully in Southeast Asia over the centuries, but the existing rivalry could become more serious as both grow stronger and seek spheres of influence.

India also feels threatened by Chinese efforts in the Middle East. It is especially concerned over China's supplying missiles and other materiel to Saudi Arabia and its help to other Middle East nations.

India has based its strategy for dealing with the Chinese threat on a combination of military and diplomatic approaches. It has directly addressed the threat by forming and training ten mountain divisions for high-altitude warfare against the Chinese, and it has trained its Air Force, which was not ready in 1962, for operating at high land altitudes. The Air Force can play a key role against extended Chinese supply routes. These forces, however, can only delay a major Chinese attack.

On the diplomatic front, India developed closer relations with the Soviet Union to balance China's relationship with Pakistan. The Treaty of Friendship in 1971 called for consultation between India and the Soviet Union in a crisis and generally accomplished India's aim of neutralizing China. The treaty, renewed in 1991, now applies to Russia.[20]

Thanks to the end of the cold war and the changed world situation, India faces new and complex problems, but also the possibility of restoring relations with China. Somewhat improved Russo-Chinese interaction might weaken Russian support for India, but the opportunity for better Indian relations with China might reduce India's need for Russian support. In fact, Moscow has encouraged India to improve ties with China.

Prime Minister Li Peng's six-day visit to New Delhi in December 1991, the first by a Chinese prime minister in 31 years, seemed to herald new interaction. While no major issues were resolved, the friendly and constructive approach on both sides should help with the problems and obstacles separating the two nations. Li Peng agreed that India and China should work together for regional peace, stability, and development. The two sides reiterated their adherence to the five principles agreed to in 1954 and expressed the hope that the meeting would usher in a new era in their relationship.

Great differences remain, however, in the ideology and the goals of Beijing and New Delhi in South Asia, and both must overcome a long

---

[20]Indo-Soviet relations are discussed immediately below, in this section.

period of mistrust.[21] China's unilateral declaration of sovereignty over the islands of the South and East China seas, its activities in Burma, and its nuclear explosion in June 1992 did nothing to reassure India.

THE SOVIET UNION

Generally hostile relations between India and China since the late 1950s, and the latter's increasing support of Pakistan, have caused India to turn more and more to the Soviet Union for friendship and aid. India's relationship with the USSR came easily and naturally, as Nehru and other early Indian leaders had long admired the Soviets and their way to development as a model for other undeveloped nations, though many did not wholly approve of the Soviet political system.

The USSR and China developed a rift in the 1950s and Pakistan became involved in the U.S. anti-Soviet network of alliances. The Soviets supported India's takeover of Goa in 1961, the Indian position on Kashmir, and its opposition to the transfer of U.S. arms to Pakistan.

In 1968, the Soviets indicated their willingness to sign a formal treaty of friendship with India, and a draft treaty was negotiated by late 1970. India was reluctant to sign, however, partially because it feared that doing so might jeopardize its nonaligned foreign policy. Moreover, the Indian public was not ready for such a move.

Pakistani-Chinese relations became increasingly close in the late 1960s, and the internal situation in East Pakistan worsened during the same period as the government of Yahya Khan in Karachi cracked down on the independence fighters in the east and hundreds of thousands of East Pakistanis (Bengalis) fled to West Bengal. In early 1971, Indira Gandhi decided to intervene in East Pakistan in support of the guerrilla independence movement. At the same time, India turned increasingly to the Soviet Union because of (1) the approaching crisis in East Pakistan, (2) Henry Kissinger's visit to Beijing in July 1971, which Pakistan helped to facilitate and which suggested closer U.S.-PRC ties, and (3) the possibility of U.S. and Chinese aid to Pakistan.

---

[21]For an excellent summary of Indo-Chinese relations, see Surjit Mansingh, "An Overview of India-China Relations: From When to Where," *Indian Defence Review,* 1992, pp. 70–78.

The Soviet Union, however, declined to back India on the East Pakistan issue and urged a peaceful settlement. Mrs. Gandhi—either to improve relations with China so as to forestall its possible support of Pakistan, or to gain Soviet support—made some friendly gestures to Beijing that the latter did not reciprocate. The gestures sufficed, however, to make the Soviets choose India over Pakistan. India and the USSR finally signed a Treaty of Peace, Friendship, and Cooperation on August 9, 1971, in New Delhi, about a month after Kissinger's trip to China.

The Soviets stopped sending arms to Pakistan and warned China that it would not tolerate any intervention on behalf of Pakistan in East Pakistan. At the same time, Soviet submarines in the Indian Ocean reminded the Americans of the Soviet friendship with India. The Soviets saw the treaty as a first step toward Brezhnev's goal of a cooperative security pact with Asia. The Soviets also believed that India could be a helpful friend in world councils, particularly at the UN and in the nonaligned movement.

The Soviet-Indian treaty was not, however, an alliance; in fact, over the next 20 years, each government interpreted the treaty to serve its own interests at any given time, emphasizing the treaty's economic, political, or security aspects as it suited them. The Indian friendship with the Soviet Union, begun even before the treaty consolidated it, lasted for over 30 years and will doubtless continue with Russia and the Central Asian republics.

India and the Soviets did not agree on all matters. India, for example, albeit rather quietly, opposed the Soviet invasion of Hungary in 1956 and of Afghanistan in 1979. India only mildly disapproved the presence of the Soviet fleet in the Indian Ocean, but loudly protested that of the U.S. fleet. It never accepted Brezhnev's or Gorbachev's ideas of a collective security pact in Asia.

As trade between the USSR and India increased and the former supplied arms to the latter, relations grew closer. India nevertheless has maintained its independence, never allowing Soviet military personnel on its military bases. And despite Moscow's urging, it has refused to sign the nonproliferation treaty.

The two nations have, however, shared many of the same interests and goals, and were circumspect when they did not. Both opposed colonialism and, as they saw it, the American version of it. Both have been seriously concerned about China as a security threat (though at brief intervals seeking better relations with the Chinese), and they have developed close and mutually beneficial trade relations. Some agreement on ideological considerations (i.e., socialism) and cultural and other exchanges have contributed to a continuing friendly relationship.

The sudden demise of the Soviet Union has shocked Indians and in some ways left them feeling unprotected.[22] Although the Soviet-Indian friendship treaty was not an alliance, Indians considered the Soviet nuclear capability a protection against the Chinese and the Americans. India now seeks to improve relations with both the United States and, though not at the same pace, with China. It is also reaching out for broader contacts throughout the world, including Turkey, Southeast Asia, and Israel.

India has not forsaken Russia, which it sees as largely replacing the Soviet Union, and they renewed the friendship treaty in 1991. India gave a million tons of grain to help the Soviet Union in the same year, and Indians still talk of their long and fruitful friendship with the Soviets. India wants to continue its relationship with Russia, as well as with other parts of the former Soviet Union, especially the Central Asian republics. It sees Russia as an important country and one that still has nuclear weapons. Indians believe that Russia will eventually be able to help counter the unipolarity of the world, which Indians abhor, and they intend to continue to cultivate their relationship with Russia.[23]

BEYOND SOUTH ASIA: THE INDIAN OCEAN REGION

India sees the Indian Ocean as a vital frontier, along with the northwest and northeast land boundaries (see Figure 3, above). Until the late 1960s, the Royal Navy defended India from the sea. Its departure in 1967, when Britain withdrew from east of Suez, left the Indians feeling vulnerable and unprotected. They felt even more so when the United States gained a base at Diego Garcia (see Figure 3, above) and both superpowers sent naval ships into the Indian Ocean.

Indian admirals like to remind the government that Britain—the one power to subjugate India from afar—had come by sea and that such an invasion should not be allowed to happen again. India now be-

---

[22]Having been ruled over and protected for so long by the Moghuls and the British, Indians tend to feel insecure and surrounded by hostile states when they do not have a protector. The collapse of the Soviet Union has again raised fears and insecurity and accounts to some extent for India's rapprochement with the United States.

[23]A. P. Venkateshwaran, "To End with a Whimper," *Indian Defence Review,* January 1992, p. 23. See also the report on Russo-Indian cooperation in manufacturing weapons, *Washington Times,* June 17, 1992, p. A2.

lieves that it should have defensive forces in the Indian Ocean to keep hostile powers at bay and protect its maritime interests. India would like a 360-degree *cordon sanitaire.*

India has many specific concerns about the Indian Ocean region, including its strategic competition with Pakistan and China, discussed above. This competition extends to both the Middle East and Southeast Asia, and even to Africa and the Indian Ocean island states. New Delhi raised an alarm when China sold IRBM missiles to Saudi Arabia, arguing that this represented a further encirclement of India by Beijing.

Other concerns stem from Indian fears, partially a legacy of the colonial era, but also a result of postindependence experience, that powerful outside states will establish a presence in the Indian Ocean area, perhaps in collusion with weaker regional states.

In the seventies and eighties, India feared that the United States, usually seen as unfriendly to India, was becoming a major hostile power in the area by virtue of the U.S. acquisition of a base on Diego Garcia and the presence in the Indian Ocean of large elements of the U.S. fleet.[24] Soviet naval deployments seemed to suggest a superpower confrontation in the region and possible military activities. With the end of the cold war, both powers have reduced their presence and the threat of superpower conflict has almost disappeared.

Now, however, relative military superiority of the United States in the area, as demonstrated by Operation Desert Storm, concerns the Indians. Though the Indian government has voiced no strong objections, as it feels an improving relationship with the United States lessens the American threat, some Indians are nevertheless wary of an American presence: In the first place, they distrust Washington's uneven record of support for New Delhi; second, they have consistently opposed an American presence in the Indian Ocean region. Anti-American feeling remains widespread in India, though the government seems eager to improve relations.[25]

Indians also worry about the arrival of foreign navies in the Indian Ocean at some future time. Indian naval advocates especially fear a Chinese naval presence in the area and, in the more distant future,

---

[24]The Indians imposed limitations on Sri Lanka's use of Trincomalee harbor in the 1987 agreement out of fear that the United States might gain the use of it.

[25]The United States has historically been India's largest aid donor and it provided some military and political support to New Delhi in the 1962 war with China. However, Washington gave aid to neither side during the 1965 India-Pakistan war, and it overtly opposed New Delhi in the 1971 war, which led to the creation of Bangladesh.

the possible return of Japanese forces. India would much prefer a *Pax Indica* in the Indian Ocean, with little or no outside naval presence.

India has special interests in the Middle East and West Asia, especially in the Persian Gulf region, as well as security concerns:

- New Delhi hopes to become a source of finished products, goods, and advanced engineering and construction services, not merely a source of cheap labor or a subcontractor to Western multinationals.
- India depends on the Middle East for a large percentage of its oil. However, many likely oil suppliers are orthodox Islamic states that have regularly criticized New Delhi for its treatment of Indian Muslims and for India's control over part of Kashmir. Only Iraq supported India on Kashmir.
- Several Islamic fundamentalist Arab states have funded militant Indian Muslim groups.

Members of the Indian strategic community often express a sense of being surrounded by a sea of Islamic fanatics and argue that India and the United States have a common interest in containing militant Islam. There seems to be no real Muslim strategic threat to Indian security, but psychologically the Muslim presence revives Indian feelings of being encircled by hostile, especially Islamic, forces.[26]

The Indian government, in a change of policy, normalized its relationship with Israel in 1992, and the two countries will exchange ambassadors. India has not, however, severed ties with the Palestine Liberation Organization (PLO) and Iraq.

The overseas Indian communities, which stretch from Fiji in the east to South Africa in the west, have concerned both Indian politicians and the Indian public. India has vigorously opposed apartheid in South Africa. Only in recent years, however, has India even come close to acquiring the military capability to think about protecting such communities. The persecution of Indian minorities in Sri Lanka and Fiji, a powerful human rights issue throughout India, could well serve as a stimulus for sustaining power-projection capabilities.

India feels that it has good relations with the nations of Southeast Asia and points with pride to the influence of Indian culture on the

---

[26]Some officials do not fear Muslim encirclement. For example, Secretary of External Affairs Dixit said on a visit to Washington in April 1992 that he did not consider the Muslims a threat.

area. It also has an interest in the Strait of Malacca, which Indonesia, Malaysia, and Singapore dominate (see Figure 3, above). Some Indians speak of an informal coalition of India, Indonesia, and Vietnam to keep peace in the region and, not incidentally, to contain China's ambitions in the area.

India admires and envies the tremendous economic growth of the ASEAN states, as well as the ASEAN cooperative mechanism. But while India is giving these neighbors somewhat more attention than formerly, they do not bulk large in Indian thinking.

Among the Southeast Asian states, however, Burma deserves special mention. It is the only South Asian state to have a land border with India, though the border is a long distance and a difficult journey from central India, and some Burmese tribes inhabit both sides of the border. The British conquered Burma in the nineteenth century with the essential help of Indian troops. The British brought in Indian labor and administrators, and Indians soon became a powerful factor in the Burmese economy.

The Burmese rioted against the Indians in the 1930s and anti-Indian feelings have been high at times. In 1961, General Ne Win of Burma expelled 200,000 natives of the subcontinent (they had lived in Burma since before the partition, so they were neither Indian nor Pakistani) and confiscated their properties. The Burmese permitted cross-border aid to the Nagas and other tribes rebelling against the Indian government in northeastern India and allowed the rebels sanctuary in Burma.

India, for its part, has opposed the State Law and Order Restoration Council (SLORC), the military regime that took over the Burmese government in 1988. India broadcast anti-SLORC programs on All-India Radio, a practice that SLORC much resented. India also openly supports the democratic opposition.

All nations but China have cut off aid to this repressive military regime. The Chinese, with the agreement of the Burmese, have opened the Sino-Burmese border in the north to the free flow of goods. Having also provided considerable aid and a billion dollars' worth of military assistance to northern Burma, China has essentially established economic hegemony in that part of the country, increased its influence over the Burmese government, and established close relations with the Burmese military.

The Chinese are rumored to be seeking better access to the Bay of Bengal by improving roads from the north to Rangoon, and they have offered to improve harbor facilities in the city. Pakistan, China's long-time friend, is also believed to be providing unspecified assistance to the Burmese military regime.

The Thai are concerned about the expanded Chinese influence in Burma, traditionally a nation of special interest to Thailand. At Emperor Hirohito's funeral in February 1989, Thai Prime Minister Chatchai called on President Bush to expand relations with Vietnam and Burma, as he feared too much Chinese influence was developing in the latter.

All of these changes disturb India, and one Indian has written that it is part of an encirclement of India led by the Chinese.[27] Other than to protest and to wage psychological operations against the SLORC, India probably cannot do much. The friendly visit of Chinese Prime Minister Li Peng to India in December 1991 contrasts with China's unfriendly behavior elsewhere in India's neighborhood.

The other Southeast Asian states do not see the situation exactly as the Indians do, but rather share some of the concerns and anxieties of India's closer neighbors. Some wonder about Indian intentions in the Andaman Islands (see Figure 1, above), what actions India might undertake with a large navy, and how India would behave should the United States withdraw from the region.[28] Several local states want to obtain surveillance aircraft for use in the Indian Ocean.

Indians speak of their country's peaceful cultural influence in Southeast Asia, but India's military buildup raises suspicions that India's interests may not be peaceful. Indians living in these states might also attract the attention of India if they were perceived as being mistreated. On the surface, relations between India and Southeast Asia generally appear good, but the smaller states are genuinely concerned about India's military power and what it proposes to do with that power.[29]

Strategically, India aspires to serve as a friendly regional peacekeeper. It sees itself as a benevolent nation and a friendly policeman that seeks peace and stability for the entire Indian Ocean region. It denies any hegemonic designs or territorial ambitions. It vehemently rejects and resents charges of being a regional bully. It wants not

---

[27]Mansingh, 1992, p. 75.

[28]Some Indians realize that Southeast Asians, though otherwise friendly, are concerned about the Indian buildup. See Professor P. K. Singh, "Maritime Security of India," *USI Journal*, October–December 1990, p. 423.

[29]Australia shares these concerns. Part of the problem stems from the failure of the Indian government to clearly state its naval strategy.

46

only to play the role of friendly peacekeeper but also to be acknowledged and endorsed in that role by others, especially the great powers.

In sum, while they may disagree on particulars, virtually the entire Indian strategic community is united in the belief that others have not recognized New Delhi's legitimate regional role. India sees itself as the preeminent power in the region, though not an authoritarian one. At the same time, New Delhi has never fully articulated its strategy or policies for the region. Indians were pleased at American support for their operation in Sri Lanka and the Maldives, but wonder about the firmness of such support for India's longer-term regional role and aspirations.

INDIA AND THE WORLD

The Indian strategic community is one of the few in the world that aspires to a global role. As best expressed in Nehru's writings, Indians have always seen their country as an international player and contributor to a new world order. This broader vision is a major factor in shaping Indian relations with the United States and other major powers.

Shortly after independence, Nehru wrote: "India is going to be and is bound to be a country that counts in world affairs, not I hope in a military sense, but in many other senses, which are more important and effective in the end."[30] Indians today still emphasize the idea that although they have no territorial ambitions, a state as large and important as India should be heard and respected in world councils.

Nehru recognized the linkage between domestic weakness and a global role in the 1950s, observing that "any part we want to play in world affairs depends entirely on internal strength, unity, and conditions of our country."[31] He understood that others would pay attention to India in proportion to its strength—and not necessarily its military strength; his policies of self-reliance clearly indicate this awareness, as did his early concentration on developing a sound economy.

Indian nationalists believe that India has always been a great country, even though it has rarely been united or militarily powerful. Since the late nineteenth century, they have argued that India's size,

---

[30]Nehru, 1983, p. 47.
[31]Ibid., p. 70.

population, strategic location, and culture constitute an obvious basis for India's standing as a great world nation.[32] Nehru could not imagine that the world would not accord India its rightful position.

But the world has not accorded India its rightful position in the eyes of most of the Indian political and strategic community. Indians brush aside the typical foreign view—that India lacks historical and political continuity and coherence and that it is a land of poverty—as stemming from ignorance of the powerful unity produced by India's rich culture.

At independence, most Indians saw the beginning of a new and glorious period for their country. Nehru's famous speech of August 14, 1947, "A Tryst with Destiny," reflected this pride and expectation.[33] Even recent critics of Nehru (who believe he was too soft on Pakistan and China) argue that India was fortunate to have had such a world-renowned leader. They appreciate the way he applied India's spiritual and moral tradition to world affairs.

Nehru believed that a nation's foreign policy had to reflect and express its values and that pluralistic, democratic, and secular India was destined to play a principled, moral role in world affairs. Nehru asserted this belief in his espousal of Pan-Asianism and nonalignment, his frequent criticism of the use of force to settle disputes between nations, and his strong support for the United Nations, at least in its early years.

Nonalignment became the essential basis of Nehru's foreign policy. This policy, though much misunderstood and maligned, has served India well. It avoided entangling alliances and joining either bloc. It rested on neither neutrality nor passivity, nor did it place India equidistant between the blocs, as President Eisenhower mistakenly believed. Nehru detested the cold war and what he called the "bloc mentality." His was essentially a policy of independence, of doing what he thought was best for India, of keeping India free of dependence on any other authority. It was, in many ways, a pragmatic policy.

Nehru conceived of Indian interests in the context of world peace. Understanding that the first duty of a country is to protect itself, he put India's interests first. However, his pursuit of India's interests—

---

[32]I use the term "world nation" to mean a nation that counts importantly in the world, but does not rank as a world power and cannot project military power throughout the world.

[33]See Nehru, 1983.

for example, his China policy—was sometimes unrealistic. He is best remembered for his eloquent espousal of the idealistic goals of peace, world cooperation, anticolonialism, racial equality, and Pan-Asianism.

No other newly independent nation arrived on the world scene with the likes of Nehru to lead it. His wise and realistic policy of independent action, or nonalignment, proved to be exactly what this great, but young and militarily weak, nation needed. He gave India a stature in the world that it has not enjoyed since his death.[34]

After World War II, all of the colonies in Asia began to achieve independence, a shared goal after the shared experience of colonialism for most. Nehru believed in and tried to lead a Pan-Asian movement. Asia, he said, had come alive. He held conferences and meetings and talked about the "new spirit of Asia," Asian sentiment, and Asian cooperation. Unfortunately, the euphoria of Indian independence blinded him to the great differences in ethnic composition, culture, history, geographical position, and interests of the various new Asian nations.

Furthermore, many in India and elsewhere did not share Nehru's broad vision of Asia. This vision was shaken by the Chinese takeover of Tibet in 1950 and abruptly destroyed by the Chinese invasion of India in 1962. Asians turned out not to be one homogeneous group, all believing in peace and cooperation. Pan-Asianism was not a practical concept. To Nehru's credit, he learned his lesson: He realized, though somewhat late, that India must have powerful defense forces and began their development after 1962.

Indian strategists disagree as to exactly what role India should play in the world and how to reach such a goal. Senior members of the Indian strategic community, including several who worked with Nehru, insist that India's claim to world leadership must be based on moral and spiritual values. Others do not believe that a moral basis alone will enable India to achieve a world position. They argue that India must have military power and indeed must become a world military power.

Naval and nuclear advocates, especially, argue that India must have a nuclear capability and a navy able to project power.[35] The frus-

---

[34]Robert Bradnock, *India's Foreign Policy Since 1971,* Chatham House Paper, Council on Foreign Relations Press, New York, 1990, p. 17.

[35]Given India's present internal problems and severe budget constraints, these capabilities lie far in the future, but India has not given up its goals.

trations and ambitions of the nuclear hawks can be summed up by the comment of a Calcutta publisher: "Moscow and Washington can nuke Delhi, so why shouldn't Delhi have the capability to nuke them?"[36] However, some Indian thinkers appear to have come full circle and have reasserted Nehru's principle that the real basis for power in the contemporary world is economic rather than military strength.[37]

Despite the range of Indians' views on the proper global role for India, most agree that India has not received the attention or recognition it deserves. Indians strongly believe that India's size, population, history, culture, and recent achievements make India a world nation. They resent the fact that their country is not yet considered a world power, even a regional power. For many, the indifference of the world is worse than hostility. They feel a real need for world position and for the world's recognition of that position.[38]

---

[36]Interviewed by the author in Calcutta, January 1990.

[37]The present Indian ambassador to the United States, Dr. Abid Hussain, is a leading advocate of this position.

[38]The desire for world power and power-projection capabilities raises some serious questions regarding India's true intentions. Questions about this generally receive evasive answers, but I believe that Indians really do not know precisely what they want, except, in general terms, world recognition.

3. PROPOSITIONS

THE ABSENCE OF STRATEGIC THINKING

Although India has, over time, developed elements of a defense strategy, as discussed in Section 2, above, it has produced little formal strategic thinking and planning. Air Chief Marshal Suri, who heads the Indian Air Force, accurately reflected the Indian approach to strategy and planning when he characterized the Air Force as "reactive," rather than "active," adding that India had no territorial ambitions. He expressed little concern over Pakistani efforts to acquire an advanced early warning (AEW) system: "We will see how to counter it if Pakistan acquires the new capability."[1]

The lacunae in strategy and planning derive largely from India's historical and cultural development:

- First, because India has lacked political unity throughout most of its history, Indians have not thought in terms of national defense planning. The few brief periods of imperial unity depended on the will and power of a great leader, and the unity did not lead to a modern nation-state.[2] At other times, the smaller individual Indian states saw to their own local defenses.

- Second, the Hindu concept of time, or rather the lack of a sense of time—Indians view life as an eternal present, with neither history nor future—discourages planning.

- Third, Hindus consider life a mystery, largely unknowable and not entirely under man's control. In this view, fate, intuition, tradition, and emotions play important roles, but how, how much, and when is never clearly known. Man's control over his life is thus limited in Hindu eyes, and he cannot forecast or plan with any confidence.[3]

---

[1]See "Pakistan will be better armed" (interview aboard Indian Air Force plane, February 17), *Times of India* (Bombay), February 18, 1992, p. 10.

[2]Interestingly, the great Indian empires are known by the name of the dynasty: Mauryan, Gupta, and Moghul. This more personal, less national approach contrasts with that of the Roman empire, which was called the Roman empire no matter who ruled it.

[3]The remark of one senior civil servant during a discussion of how to plan for the 1962 Chinese attack on India seems to epitomize the second and third points: "Why all this [discussion]; we will see when it comes." See Steven A. Hoffman, *India and the China Crisis,* University of California Press, Berkeley, 1990, p. 254.

Aside from the Mauryan, Gupta, and Moghul empires, little historical evidence exists to suggest any sense of an Indian political entity. One finds temporary alliances of various Indian states to gain an advantage in war, but these were local agreements and in no way concerned with a greater India. The fact that Indian states almost never banded together to fight invaders suggests that they had no sense of a defense for India as a whole, only for their individual states. Many Indians told the author that their forebears identified themselves by caste, locality, and language, rather than as Indian or Hindu, which, they maintained, were Western terms.

The seeming lack of efforts toward and feelings of Indian political unity suggests that there was little thought of India even as a collection of states that might gain from some form of cooperative action or agreed-on interstate norms.[4] Broad cultural unity, however, has long existed and continues to flourish in India, though it did not, before the nationalist movement, have political attributes.

The major component of Indian unity—Hinduism—is so amorphous that Westerners have difficulty understanding how it can serve as a bond for Indians. Yet Indians consider Hinduism the primary basis for the concept of an age-old India and for the political nation of India today. Cultural history, however, is not the same as a political history, and cultural unity differs from political unity. Neither the ideal of an enduring India nor an ancient culture has had to face the myriad socioeconomic, foreign policy, and strategic problems that a political state must confront.

The British developed strategic ideas for the defense of India, but they kept the Indians out of discussions and decisions in matters of strategy. British strategic policy for the defense of India evolved over the years, and was often debated, especially between Whitehall and Delhi, but neither drew up a complete strategic plan. Indians thus had no experience with the formulation of modern strategy. As in most democracies, the British government kept a rather tight rein on the military, not allowing them to participate in the highest levels of government where strategy is sometimes considered.

---

[4]Indian history is devoid of ideas for an Indian federation comparable to Sully's Grand Design for the federation of the Christian states of Europe in the late sixteenth century. Moreover, despite the existence of some laws governing interstate and international relations, in Kautilya's view, mistrust, betrayal, and the law of the jungle characterized relations among the Indian states. See *Kautilya,* passim. See also P. Bandyopadhyay, *International Law and Custom in Ancient India,* Calcutta, 1920, S. U. Viswantha, *International Law in Ancient India,* London, 1925, and V. R. Ramachandra Dikshitar, *War in Ancient India,* Motilal Banarsidass, New Delhi, 1987.

The India of today, though based on culture, is a new and fragile political union. Large and complex problems confront it in every sphere. It cannot solve these problems on an ad hoc basis without some careful planning. While Indian culture helped make this union possible, it handicaps the union's progress by its views of time and life. Strategic thinking about this new political entity is thus a new problem.

Most Indians assert that no military or government leaders and few civil servants are directly concerned with strategic planning. India's early prime ministers, particularly Nehru and his daughter, Indira Gandhi, thought out and managed foreign policies and strategies on their own, or with a small coterie of advisers. No serious strategic planning institutions, if they ever existed, have survived in independent India, and none exists today. The recent creation of the National Security Council (NSC) acknowledges the need for strategic planning, but many Indians consider the NSC stillborn, while others believe that it will not begin to function at least for some time.

The powerful hold of India's culture notwithstanding, Indians pragmatically recognize that Western ideas are bringing changes. India will adjust to this conflict in its own way and at its own speed. With their talent for analysis and conceptualization, Indians seem admirably equipped for strategic thinking. Furthermore, as noted above, Indians do think strategically and have developed some strategic concepts, but like the British before them, they have developed these concepts in an informal and haphazard way. For example, India has never issued a white paper and does not appear inclined to do so.

Thus, the forces of culture and history and the attitude and policies of the independent Indian government have worked against the concept of strategic thinking and planning. As India's need for strategic planning increases, a structure for planning is likely to develop slowly.

INDIA ON THE STRATEGIC DEFENSIVE

Throughout most of its history, India has been on the strategic defensive. Over the centuries, armies from Central Asia and Persia have invaded the subcontinent by land, and Europeans, for a shorter period, have invaded by sea. Rarely did the Indians succeed in repulsing invaders, and they seemed not to learn from past experiences how to change this. The small Indian states concentrated more on fighting each other or assisting the invader against a rival than in turning back the invaders collectively. Indian armies seldom attempted a forward strategy against the invaders, and thus most of the fighting took place on Indian territory.

At the height of the Indian nationalists' campaign for independence in the late nineteenth and early twentieth centuries, when their sensitivities were most acute, the British India began to adopt a more passive defensive posture. Until that time, it had followed a policy ranging from offensive expansion to aggressive defense. Thus, the events of their own lifetime tended to reinforce the nationalists' perception that India historically had maintained a defensive posture and fought defensive wars.[5]

India arrived on the world scene as an independent nation and status quo power with considerable resources. The new nation inherited most of the land and resources of the subcontinent and much of the British governmental apparatus. Its goal was to hold and defend what it had. Pakistan, a much smaller nation with fewer resources, was born with an inferiority complex and with a grievance over what it considered was an unfair distribution of British assets. It was particularly upset over the loss of part of Kashmir at independence.

While India hoped that Pakistan and India would reunite, thus restoring a cultural unity and a defensible India, Pakistan preferred independence. It did not want India to enjoy its assumed superior status. Pakistan accepted the 1948 United Nations arrangement for a cease-fire line that cut Kashmir in half. India, in a defensive move, made its half an integral state of the Indian union. Pakistan took a somewhat more offensive stand: It kept its share as a territory, hoping someday to unite all of Kashmir by force or other means and to create a single Kashmiri state in Pakistan.

Since 1947, India and Pakistan have confronted each other in an almost continuous state of tension and have fought three wars. India believes that Pakistan has been the aggressor in these wars and that Islamabad continues to take the offensive with its assistance to separatist groups inside India. India considers itself constantly on the de-

---

[5]Some current military leaders complain of this defensive mentality and cite the reluctance of Indian Army leaders to develop a doctrine and tactics for armored units as an example of this defensive psyche. See Maj. Gen. Rajendra Nath, *Military Leadership in India: Vedic Period to Indo-Pakistani Wars,* Lancer Books, New Delhi, 1990, p. 379.

fensive and believes that it must keep fending off Pakistani attacks of one variety or another.[6]

Since Indian independence, China has also put India on the defensive. China seized Tibet in 1950, a move the British had worked for years to prevent. Nehru, however, did not oppose the seizure: He seemed to think that China had a right to Tibet, and he hesitated to violate the spirit of Pan-Asianism, which he held so strongly. In 1962, China revealed its hostility to India, its desire for a position in South Asia, and its willingness to take action against a fellow Asian nation by attacking India. India was not prepared and again seemed to be on the defensive.

India and China, at least for the moment, are accepting the present status quo on the border and are conducting low-level talks. India seems satisfied to hold land up to the MacMahon Line, a position it has always taken in the northeast (see Figure 1, Section 1, above). The Chinese hold the Aksai Chin salient, very important strategically to them in the northwest, but both claim the other's present holdings. India has lived with the Chinese nuclear capability for some years, seemingly without much concern.

China in many ways has behaved less provocatively than Pakistan vis-à-vis India. Furthermore, China lies outside the subcontinent and though it is India's most powerful rival, it is psychologically less of a threat to India's vital interests than Pakistan, which lies within the subcontinent. However, India has not forgotten the Chinese attack in 1962 and has prepared forces to deter, and if necessary to oppose, any renewed Chinese aggression.

THE LACK OF AN EXPANSIONIST MILITARY TRADITION

Largely because of its geography, India has a long history of nonaggression and nonexpansion outside the subcontinent. Had the Indians sought to expand to the west, north, or east, they would have faced a long, cold trek through the mountains to lands that are relatively poor and barren. Thanks to India's relative riches, however, Indians lacked an incentive to expand.

As India developed within its own boundaries, its people, especially those in the fertile northern Indo-Gangetic plain, became increasingly involved in their own internal affairs. In a few cases, they were

---

[6]At the same time, Pakistan alleges that India interferes in Sri Lanka and in Pakistan. India also acted aggressively in 1971 to split Pakistan. India is also being accused of fomenting trouble in Sind Province, Pakistan.

building great empires; in others, they were conducting interstate rivalries and small wars. At the same time, they were producing a rich and unique culture. Self-sufficient in the necessities of life, they were largely oblivious to the outside world.

The south, although often dominated by the north, was less influenced by Aryan cultural restraints and more exposed to the sea; as a result, early in Indian history it developed a significant maritime tradition. Several southern dynasties, including the Cholas, pursued an expansionist policy, particularly in Southeast Asia. The Cholas, whose short-lived empire existed nearly a thousand years ago, were the last, however, to establish colonies in what is now Malaysia and Indonesia and to fight with the local states for control of the east-west trade with China. Little maritime activity has taken place since then, until the recent naval buildup.

Independent India sees itself as continuing the tradition of nonaggression and nonexpansion outside the subcontinent. Nehru's foreign policy rested on these principles, and subsequent leaders have followed suit. The tradition of nonaggression, however, has never applied internally. Warfare within the subcontinent has been the norm for centuries. States fought to gain power and wealth, to establish empires, or to destroy them.

This seeming paradox with regard to nonaggression arises from the Indian view of the subcontinent as a single strategic area that coincides with Indian national interests. This belief justified India's taking much more active measures—some say aggressive measures—to protect its interests in the subcontinent; for example, India

- Took over Portuguese Goa in 1962 in an effort to rid itself of the last vestiges of colonialism.[7]
- Peacefully, though exerting some pressure, absorbed Sikkim in 1975.
- Actively supported the separatists in East Pakistan in 1971.
- Sent the Indian Army to defeat the Pakistani forces and to establish the new nation of Bangladesh in 1971.
- Dispatched a 50,000-man "peacekeeping force" to Sri Lanka in 1987 (but subsequently withdrew it).
- Sent forces to the Maldives (at their request) in 1988.

---

[7]Much of the motivation for this military move came from Defence Minister Krishna Menon's need to gain political support around Goa.

Most Indians see these not as aggressive moves, but rather as defensive actions to preserve India's internal security. India's neighbors, of course, take the diametrically opposite view of India's posture and actions in the subcontinent.

THE ARMY, LAND WARFARE, AND PRIMARY STRATEGIC CONCERNS

India continues to rely heavily on its Army, despite recent attention to the buildup of the Indian Navy. The Army remains the dominant military service and receives most of the defense resources.

The British, when they ruled India, developed a land-oriented defense strategy for the country. Their control of the world seas protected India from seaborne attack, but on land they were forced to contend with the Russians and Chinese for the control of Afghanistan, Iran, Central Asia, and Burma.[8]

From London, the British government, basing its power on the Royal Navy, took a global strategic view. India represented only a part of what the British empire had to protect. The Indian government, in contrast, developed a regional, land-oriented strategic view: From its perspective, the land approach presented the greatest threat.

The Indian government continues to focus on land, rather than naval, warfare. During World War II, Japan threatened India overland in the northeast. Since independence, India has fought three wars with Pakistan, primarily on the land, and one with China along the vast land border stretching from Pakistan in the west to Burma in the east. The border problems with China remain unresolved, and the Pakistanis continue to aid and abet the dissidents in Punjab and Kashmir.

In addition to protecting India's borders, the Army plays an increasingly important role in internal security. Neither the Air Force nor the Navy can contribute to this mission. In many cases, the domestic problems have exceeded the capabilities of the Indian government's civil forces to deal with them, and the government has no alternative but to call on the Army, for example, to deal with the current difficulties in Kashmir, Punjab, and Assam.

The Army does not consider these internal operations its primary responsibility, as they divert it from preparing for a real war. Army

---

[8]The Russian aspect of this contest was called the "Great Game."

---

leaders believe, however, that they must respond to civil direction. Despite the Army's attitude, some Indians are concerned that the Army may have to take control of the country if the internal disorders worsen.

The Army has evolved as an important agency of the Indian government. As an institution, it is heavily entrenched, with a momentum of its own, and it plays a powerful role in the allocation of resources. While the Navy has attracted more attention recently, the Army and the land threat will remain the preeminent concern of India in the foreseeable future, though India's new economic policies will make trade and the seas more important to India.

SELF-RELIANCE AND INDEPENDENCE

The drive for self-reliance has become an important element in the Indian strategy for attaining security, true independence, and international stature. Nehru early on came out in favor of strategic self-reliance and independence:

> In our external and internal domestic policy, in our political policy, or economic policy, we do not propose to accept anything that involves in the slightest degree dependence on any other authority.[9]

Nehru's primary foreign policy doctrine of nonalignment was intended to steer an independent course between the two superpowers. Rather than neutralism, it represented India's right to take positions in India's interest.

To ensure India's independence, Nehru emphasized the need for economic and industrial self-reliance. Even if the process proved slower and more expensive than dependence on foreign products, he believed that India must develop its own capabilities.

Just before the Chinese attack in 1962, however, Nehru brought V. K. Krishna Menon into the government as minister of defense, in part to speed up the process of achieving military self-reliance. The trickle of aid from the United Kingdom and the United States did not meet India's needs in the critical days of late 1962. Moreover, no foreign power was going to send 40 wings to defend India, as Nehru requested President Kennedy to do. Clearly, India needed to ready its own forces for action, preferably armed with Indian-made weapons.

---

[9]Nehru, 1983, p. 38.

After the Chinese attack, the Indian government initiated a vigorous military research and development program, stepped up the construction of military industries, and reequipped the Army and Air Force. Discarding long-held ideas that military expenditures degraded economic development, the government argued for a new policy of joint military and economic development that it hoped would produce synergistic effects.

India subsequently built tanks, airplanes, and ships, developed missiles, and conducted a peaceful nuclear explosion. Although much of the dual-use technology, serving both civilian and military needs, has been of good quality, India has had only limited success in producing advanced weapon systems.[10]

While seeking military and economic self-reliance, India has had to rely on outside suppliers for the most modern technology. The military demanded the best weapons and their acquisition as soon as possible. As a developing nation, India can in no way satisfy all the needs of its military for modern technology at this time.

In the 1960s, India in vain sought weapons from the United States and the United Kingdom. Unable to obtain them, it turned to the Soviet Union. In the 1970s and 1980s, India purchased and, through licensing agreements, built many Soviet weapons. It also diversified its purchases so as to avoid complete dependence on any one foreign source, buying aircraft from both France and the United Kingdom, naval vessels from Germany, and some U.S. equipment.

India continued to depend on the Soviet Union for spare parts and for some of its new weapons and equipment. Even before the Soviet Union broke up at the end of 1991, however, it was slow to fill India's orders. Indians do not know what to expect for the future.

Delhi also continues to depend on outside suppliers for many advanced-technology items, including components of the proposed light combat aircraft. It also needs computers and other sophisticated equipment from the United States, but it hopes soon to attain the capability to produce complete naval ships and other weapons with the most sophisticated and advanced components.

While Indian leaders often decry the international munitions trade, they talk of exporting weapons to spread the cost of research and development across a larger number of consumers, as well as to reduce the production costs by turning out more weapons. The demands of

---

[10]Much of the missile effort, for example, was carried out in the civil sector, although it has definite military uses.

the Indian military itself do not justify keeping open enough production lines to keep India self-reliant.[11]

India will not give up its two goals of true independence and unity unless critically important circumstances require outside support. One unknown Indian politician is reported to have said he would rather fail going it alone than survive with outside help. Self-reliance in weaponry provides the independence Indians so cherish and thus affects strategy. By reducing reliance on foreign countries, India hopes to free itself to act independently on the world scene. However, the new economic policies and military needs for high technology are undermining, though by no means destroying, this policy.

PASSIVITY IN MILITARY AFFAIRS

In addition to the factors listed at the beginning of this section— India's historical lack of political unity and the Hindu concepts of time and the mystery of life—that have contributed to the passive or reactive tendencies in Indian military matters, three others merit mention. These include the agricultural basis of Indian culture, the rigid structure of Indian society, and the bureaucracy of the Indian administrative services.

India, being a predominantly agricultural country, has a largely rural population. Like most rural people, Indian farmers have no tradition or understanding of long-range planning. For them, nature has determined the important—and unchanging—sequence of when to plant, when to harvest, etc. However, determined efforts to irrigate, fertilize, and improve seeds have created a revolution in Indian agriculture. The success of this green revolution is partially changing peasants' views. The peasant psyche remains important, however, as many of today's leaders come from the rural areas of India.[12]

Moreover, the fairly rigid and hierarchical structure of Indian society, while it does not completely stifle initiative, makes changes and individual initiative difficult. Individuals have few incentives to test the system, as failure or loss of caste is considered a calamity. Caste and family are critical, and an individual is lost outside of them.

---

[11]According to the *Asian Pacific Defence Reporter,* April 1991, p. 22, "The Indian Government has decided to liberalize the policy for defence exports under which exports of certain defence items will not require case by case clearance." The government will also, the source reports, establish a committee to sort out problems of defense exports.

[12]A large rural population is, of course, not unique to India, but this farmer attitude accounts for, or reinforces, certain cultural beliefs noted above.

Urbanization and other modern institutions are breaking down castes, but the caste riots in 1990 showed that the system retains much vitality, though it is changing and adjusting as India grapples with the problem of the development of democracy.

Finally, the Indian administrative services, especially powerful in the absence of stable political leadership at the center, react, rather than initiate. Their training, their social background, and the influence of Fabian and socialist thought does not encourage individual initiative. Strategic innovation will not come from within the traditional government bureaucracy.

STATUS AND SYMBOLISM

Status and symbolism matter greatly in Indian society, particularly in India's strategic calculations and military perceptions. Indians consider specific military capabilities—e.g., nuclear weapons, long-range missiles and aircraft, a large blue-water navy, and a strong military-industrial base—symbols of great-power status, and India therefore must have them.

Indian policymakers sometimes have difficulty explaining their intentions and plans for new weapons, especially missiles, and for expanding the Navy. This situation suggests that either they hope to obscure their long-term strategic designs or, more likely, the new weapons have not been integrated into a carefully developed strategic plan.[13] The admirals, for example, may need no further justification or rationale than that India's greatness mandates a powerful Navy. Being sensitive to status and symbols, many Indians may assume that if India had these symbols of great power it would be recognized as such.[14]

Gaining recognition of India's status in the region and in the world also plays a pivotal role in Indian strategic thought. Indeed, external recognition and validation of India's place is almost as important as actually having that status. For example, India unquestionably dominates the Indian Ocean region, but Indians are greatly frustrated by the failure of external powers to acknowledge this fact.

While the Indian government showed considerable embarrassment over the international attention to its naval buildup and insisted that

---

[13]Some Indians frankly admit that they have not thought through a strategic framework for modern weapons.

[14]I questioned several Indians about this proposition; they had not thought of it before, but after reflection some said it was probably correct.

it had no offensive designs in the region, some Indians were gratified that outsiders were beginning to pay attention to India's regional status. Outside approval of Indian actions in the Maldives and Sri Lanka especially pleased the Indians, since it implied recognition and endorsement of India's peacekeeping role and status in the region.

Indians often question why India is not a permanent member of the United Nations Security Council. At the time of independence, Nehru believed that the United States, the Soviet Union, China, and India would be the four great world states. Three of the four have permanent seats, but India does not. This clear symbol of great-power status eludes India, even though India is much larger than France and the United Kingdom and is soon to surpass them in such measures of national power as industrial, military, and economic capabilities.

Some Indian strategists now mention the possibility of cooperation with the United States in peacekeeping roles. Despite the profound differences between the two countries in economic and military strength, the strategists insist that any cooperation with the United States must be based on absolute equality. They refuse to serve under the United States. The point here is not to argue whether or not the United States and India are really equal in practical terms, but to emphasize how strongly India feels about equal status with the great powers.

THE EFFECT OF MODERN WEAPONS ON INDIAN STRATEGIC THINKING

In the absence of a strategic plan, modern military technology is beginning to shape India's strategic policy. Weapons programs are driven by technological opportunism and the institutional interests of the defense science community, not by specific strategic requirements. Indian policymakers are becoming aware of the implications of these emerging technologies and see a greater need for mechanisms to develop strategy.

Several factors in addition to its own inner dynamics are spurring India's drive toward modern military technology. First, the indigenous production of the advanced weapon systems of the great powers, Indians believe, would partially fulfill Indian ambitions for regional and world status. India seeks to keep up with Pakistan, China, and other neighbors who are ahead in or moving faster into the world of advanced military technology.

Second, Indian perceptions of its own historical inferiority in weapons feeds a "never again" attitude. India's increasing maritime interests and the need to protect them require a modern Navy. India wants to be modern and militarily strong and considers these attributes its destiny.

Third, the speed, range, precision, and devastation of modern weapons systems are rapidly changing the nature of war and making the traditional Indian strategic posture more difficult. The Gulf war showed clearly the enormous power of offensive weapons. Advanced armor, precision guided missiles, long-range missiles, and modern aircraft will require Delhi to revise its defensive concepts.[15] The Indians, already alert to the need for modern weapons, see this need even more clearly now.

India has three options for defense against its main threat, Pakistan:

- First, it can pursue its traditional defensive strategy of guarding the border with mobile reserves.
- Second, it can develop strong enough forces to deter a Pakistani attack.
- Third, it can preempt.

Under the first option, Pakistan might plan a quick surprise blitz with immediate territorial gains, hoping that world opinion would soon halt the war, with Pakistan holding the gains. These would be powerful bargaining chips for subsequent peace negotiations. In a longer war, India's greater staying power and mobile reserves would probably prevail. Because this second possibility is less likely, India would have to develop a more effective and immediate defense.

The second option would require forces strong enough to deter any Pakistani attack. To be credible in Pakistan, these forces must convince the Pakistanis that they would lose any war that they started. Deterrence, however, is delicate; it can change rapidly with the introduction of new weapons, shifts in alliances, and the perceived changes of will on the part of Indian or Pakistani leaders.

The third and boldest option would involve preemption. In this case, India would attack Pakistani forces before they could launch an attack. The decision to preempt depends on good intelligence and the capability for rapid execution. Whether General Sundarji's Operation

---

[15]Current technology developments will undoubtedly change both land and naval warfare drastically in the next few decades.

Brass Tacks maneuvers in 1987 constituted a bold exercise or the beginning of a preemptive attack on Pakistan was not clear at the time. Few in the Indian Army are as bold as Sundarji, but technology is driving the Indians to review their strategic posture and it will likely lead to a more active defense posture in the future.

It is not a great leap from an offensive defense or preemption to thinking offensively. This is not to suggest that India has any specific offensive intentions or goals, but some modern weapons encourage offensive thinking. But irrespective of whether the Indian leadership is thinking offensively, India is developing a capacity to execute offensive military actions.

India has twice (the second time in June 1992) successfully launched the Agni intermediate-range ballistic missile (IRBM), which has a range of about 1500 miles and could reach the Middle East, China, and Southeast Asia.[16] If produced and deployed, the Agni would give India the capability for deterrence or for a preemptive first strike in a large radius around India. In addition, technological advances in naval platforms and weapons have extended India's reach into the Indian Ocean for both a forward defense and limited power projection.

The Indian Air Force has transport aircraft that could rapidly move a battalion or more. Furthermore, India carried out an amazingly effective airlift early in the Gulf crisis, when aircraft of the civilian A320 Airbus fleet airlifted about 150,000 Indians out of the Middle East in about three weeks, approximately the same as the number of troops that the United States was flying in.

Both India and Pakistan seem close to attaining a nuclear weapons capability. In fact, Pakistan claims that it has such a capability. Although China already produces these weapons, India seems less concerned at the moment about China's intentions than about Pakistan's.[17] The latter's acquisition of a nuclear weapons capability will almost surely trigger an overt Indian program, if it has not already done so. The possibility of acquiring nuclear weapons is already stimulating debates on nuclear strategies for South Asia. Participants in these debates often cite the long peace between the

---

[16]The Integrated Guided Missile Development Program (IGMDP), building on older civilian space programs, has developed a family of missiles that could cover the entire region and, of course, carry nuclear warheads. This indigenous missile program has popular support. The Agni test is referred to officially as a technological demonstration.

[17]China's large nuclear explosion in June 1992, while the president of India was visiting there, may change India's view of the Chinese.

superpowers—peace that they attribute to nuclear balance—as a reason for India and Pakistan to have a nuclear capability. Whether nuclear weapons would stabilize or destabilize is a major unanswered question.[18]

THE NAVY

The role and objectives of the Indian Navy are eliciting considerable discussion inside and outside India.[19] Most Indians consider the Indian Ocean India's third important frontier (the northeast and the northern are the first and second), and they argue that India needs its Navy to protect itself from outside aggression. Indians also see the need to safeguard India's increasing maritime interests, including:

- Its trade routes and ships
- Its access to Middle East oil
- Its extended economic zone
- Its pioneer status under the Law of the Seas for the potential mineral exploration of a large area in the Indian Ocean and similar interest in the Antarctic region
- Its islands in the Bay of Bengal and the Arabian Sea
- Its close relations with Mauritius and the Seychelles (see Figure 2, Section 1, above)

---

[18]The Lawrence Livermore National Laboratories in California are exploring this question. See also *Nuclear Proliferation in South Asia: The Prospects for Arms Control,* a report prepared for Los Alamos National Laboratory, edited by Stephen Philip Cohen, Westview Press, Boulder, Colorado, 1991.

[19]The considerable literature on the Navy includes several articles by Ashley Tellis: "Banking on Deterrence," *Naval Proceedings,* March 1988, pp. 148–152; "India's Naval Expansion: Reflections on History and Strategy," *Comparative Strategy,* Vol. 8, No. 2, 1987, pp. 185–219; "Securing the Barracks: The Logic, Structure and Objectives of India's Naval Expansion," Department of Political Science, University of Chicago, unpublished and undated; "New Acquisitions on the Indian Subcontinent," *Naval Forces,* Vol. 11, No. 1, 1990. Admiral R. H. Tahiliana, interview, *Indian Defence Review,* July 1988, pp. 16–21, and "Maritime Strategy for the 90's," *Indian Defence Review,* July 1989, pp. 19–30. See also Admiral H. N. Kohli, "The Geopolitical and Strategic Considerations that Necessitate the Expansion and Modernization of the Indian Navy," *Indian Defence Review,* January 1989, pp. 33–46; and Professor P. K. Singh, "Maritime Security of India," *USI Journal,* October–December 1990, pp. 414–425. K. M. Pannikar, *Problems of Indian Defense,* New York, 1985, pp. 105–114, an old but excellent discussion of India's defense problems. *Indian Defence Review,* July 1990, has several articles on the Navy.

- Its considerable interest in the choke points of the Indian Ocean, including the Red Sea, the Strait of Malacca, and the Madagascar region (see Figure 3, Section 1, above).

Indian naval proponents hesitate to discuss specific threats; instead, they emphasize the broad range of India's maritime interests as adequate justification for a large navy. They note also that a great India requires a large navy to carry out its regional responsibilities.[20]

Naval proponents do, however, discuss threats in a general way. They point out the high mobility of navies and note that a hostile threat may develop in the Indian Ocean with little warning. Smaller states, including Pakistan, can and do, without informing India, invite the great powers to send naval ships into the Indian Ocean so as to counter Indian power. Future threats that may arise from China, Japan, and other nations, naval proponents say, must be anticipated now, as it takes a long time to build ships and develop the infrastructure to support them.

The presence of naval ships of the great powers, especially the American naval buildup in the Indian Ocean and the acquisition of a base on Diego Garcia aroused Indian fears in the 1970s, though neither was directed against India. In late 1971, however, the foray of the *USS Enterprise* into the Bay of Bengal to show support for Pakistan after India's victory reminded Indians of the threat from the sea. As a result, the Indian government has paid greater attention to the Navy, instituting a program for its modernization and expansion.

The Navy at present has two old carriers, 19 conventional submarines (the leased nuclear submarine was returned to the Soviet Union), 25 destroyers and frigates, 27 patrol and coastal ships, and 41 combat aircraft including Sea Harriers and TU-142 Bear F surveillance aircraft.[21] This fleet dwarfs the navies of the other 40-odd states on the Indian Ocean periphery and appears to dominate the region, except for the presence of the great-power naval forces.

The Indian Navy also attracts the attention of India's neighbors, who see it as an instrument of Indian power projection and ambitions to

---

[20]Admiral J. G. Nadkarni, formerly chief of the Navy staff, and Eric Gonsalves, formerly secretary of the External Affairs Ministry, have both made this point. See editorial, *USI Journal,* October–December 1990, p. 413.

[21]*Asian Pacific Defence Reporter,* 1991 Annual Reference Edition, December 1990–January 1991, pp. 146–147.

dominate the Indian Ocean region. However, a careful look at the Navy—the carriers for instance—reveals a limited power-projection capability against even modest opposition. Secretary of Defence Naresh Chandra said in January 1990 that he was lucky to have one of these old carriers operational on any given day.[22] The carriers' small complement of Harriers and helicopters—six to eight of each—gives the carriers only a short power-projection range, and problems of logistic support limit time on station away from port.[23]

Now that the cold war is over and the United States is reducing its presence in the Indian Ocean, the Indians see new problems. The U.S. withdrawal will likely create a vacuum that will add to the Indian leaders' uncertainties. They wonder whether other outside powers will move into the region, or whether other regional powers will develop navies to fill the vacuum. India, as the great and democratic nation of the region, considers itself bound by duty and responsibility to fill this vacuum.

India's new and wider-ranging maritime interests, as well as the protection of India itself, pose new challenges for the Navy in the modern technological age. The rapidly changing political world also poses new challenges and opportunities. In a sense, the Navy is constrained by neither the conservative traditions of land defense nor the restrictions that land frontiers impose on the Army.[24] The Navy, having come of age as major technological advances were made in naval warfare, is more likely than the Army to meet modern problems with modern technology and to face future challenges with greater boldness.

This is not to suggest that naval officers have shed all their culture, for they have not; however, the pragmatic side of the Indian often comes to the fore in such situations. Naval officers may have a greater appreciation of modern weapons than the officers of the other services, but the Gulf war has made all military officers more aware

---

[22]Interview, January 18, 1990, New Delhi. Chandra also said that he had heard much talk of a blue-water navy, but he would be happy to have a clear-water navy.

[23]Talk of India's power projection seems exaggerated; however, neither the Indian Navy nor plans for its future should be underestimated.

[24]The Indian admirals may silently remember the Royal Navy's contribution to British India's security through control of the seas, but they speak openly of the European arrival by sea and the subsequent "enslavement" of India. Had the Moghuls only recognized the naval threat and developed a Navy, they argue, India might have had a quite different history.

of the importance and power of modern weapons. This awareness will undoubtedly initiate serious rethinking of strategy.[25]

No authoritative government statement exists on Indian naval strategy. Several regional states attribute to India a desire for regional hegemony; some Indians would also state this as their goal and would seek to acquire power-projection capabilities for the Navy.[26] Yet most members of the Indian strategic community contend that the Navy is only one part of India's defensive posture in the region. Given India's budgetary problems, the government is unlikely to increase the size of the Navy as planned. The Navy will, however, remain a dominant force in the region.

THE COMPLEXITIES AND PARADOXES OF INDIAN STRATEGIC THINKING

In this effort to identify and distill the main characteristics of India's strategy and strategic thinking, I have had to resort to considerable simplification. Complexity, not simplicity, however, is the norm for India. I shall therefore review briefly, again oversimplifying, the major complexities and contradictions that characterize Indian strategy and strategic thinking.

- No formal efforts or institutions of government exist to develop strategies for India, but on an ad hoc and pragmatic basis, Indians have produced the strategies and policies discussed above.

- Military and economic power exist side by side with widespread and abject poverty. Indians see poverty as a condition of life and maintain that it has nothing to do with military might. However, Indians are increasingly concerned with the poor and downtrodden.

- Indians are often assertive in their views and positions; at the same time, their strategic thinking tends to be defensive.

- Although the Indian government denies that it is seeking power in the international hierarchy, many of its actions are seen as contributing to the aggrandizement of its power.

---

[25]*USI Journal,* January–March 1991, is devoted largely to the need for new thinking and improved government capabilities.

[26]The perception of a powerful and expanding Indian Navy could trigger a naval race in the region as the smaller states, especially in Southeast Asia, try to develop defenses against it. Several ASEAN states, for example, have asked that surveillance aircraft be used in the Indian Ocean, and have discussed new naval facilities in the area.

- India argues for the legal and moral equality of all nations, yet it looks down on smaller states and seeks a permanent seat on the UN Security Council.

- Indians are proud and extremely sensitive. They believe that India merits international status by virtue of its culture, size, population, achievements since independence, and especially its democracy, and they resent being ignored and undervalued by the important nations of the world despite these attributes. Yet Indians appear insensitive to the feelings of their smaller neighbors and seem to ignore the simple fact that the size of their country alone elicits feelings of insecurity in the region.

- Indians tend to be suspicious, fearful of betrayal, and envious of their neighbors; yet they value truth and spiritual morality.

- Indians esteem their past empires, and the Indian elite is alleged to have inherited the "imperial" mind-set of the British. India nevertheless ranks among the world's most strident anti-imperialists, as it decries the oppressiveness and evil of Western colonialism.

- Indians can be expedient and pragmatic in their foreign policies and strategies, but they like to emphasize the moral and spiritual aspects of India.

- Hinduism is one of the most tolerant and encompassing beliefs in the world, yet today one finds so-called fundamentalist—or, more accurately, militant and fanatical—Hindus. Westerners have difficulty understanding how adherents of this tolerant, diverse religion can adopt fundamentalist positions, and most Indians believe that the word fundamentalism does not apply to Hindus.

- India is culturally old but politically young. It reveres its old, unifying culture; at the same time, it is struggling with serious separatist problems.

- India would like to be the friendly peacekeeper of the Indian Ocean, but it is building up its military power to dominate the region.

- Indians feel proud and strong yet insecure and encircled by hostile forces. India's growing strength reassures them, but they fear the spreading Islamic fundamentalism that surrounds them and the uncertainty of the post-cold-war world.

- Indians are fiercely independent, but their fear of encirclement almost demands that they have powerful friends, such as the British and the Soviets. They seem somewhat lost without the Soviets, but they are trying to maintain good relations with Russia and are courting the United States.

- Much is changing in India, but much remains the same. Indians are quick to accept the modern materialistic life, but deep within they retain many old and basic beliefs. They consider culture the basis for modern Indian national political identity, but giving it up yet retaining Indian identity poses serious problems and tensions.

4. THE ROLE OF THE MILITARY

Since independence, the Indian government has exercised extremely tight civilian control over the military.[1] Most democracies follow this policy, including the British, who ruled India and commanded the Indian Army before independence. India has pursued the policy to a point where the military have almost no input at all in the formulation of higher defense policy and national strategy.

Nehru had a rather strong antimilitary attitude, most likely based, first and foremost, on his respect and affection for Gandhi and his successful nonviolent independence campaign. Other factors probably included Nehru's contacts with Fabian socialists, most of whom were pacifists; his great admiration for the pacifist emperor Ashoka; and the fact that the Army did not take part in the nationalist movement. Nehru gave top priority to peaceful coexistence and nonalignment to ensure world peace; he wanted India to pursue economic development with all its effort and resources. He neglected the military, giving it few resources, and downgraded its top leadership in the Warrant of Precedence, while increasing the status and pay of both civil servants and the police.

As a matter of fact, the Army believed that it had contributed to independence. Immediately after World War II, the Army experienced several mutinies. In the view of the military, the mutinies suggested to the British that some of the unrest in India had seeped into the military. The realization that they might not be able to count on the Indian Army thus weakened the British resolve to fight to keep India.[2] The Army also liked to point out that it had played a role in persuading the few recalcitrant princely states to join the Indian union in 1947–1948, had successfully defended Kashmir from the Pakistanis, and had helped the thousands of refugees after partition. It considered itself a loyal participant in the new Indian union.

Nevertheless, Nehru often refused to accept advice or counsel from the military leadership, sometimes rather dramatically. In 1951, General Cariappa, then commander in chief of the Indian Army, warned the minister of defense of a possible Chinese threat to India

---

[1]The military are also physically separated from civilian society and kept in cantonments away from the public eye. Even on internal security missions, they usually operate in the background, behind the police and paramilitary forces.

[2]Rajesh Kadian, *India and Its Army,* Vision Books, New Delhi, 1990, p. 41.

after the Chinese had taken over Tibet; Cariappa urged that defensive actions be taken in the northeast. On the defense minister's recommendation, Cariappa also briefed the prime minister on these recommended defensive measures. Nehru asked why these measures were needed; Cariappa replied that the Chinese might have designs on this region of India. At this point, Nehru said:

> It is not the business of the Commander in Chief to tell the Prime Minister who is going to attack us where. In fact, the Chinese will defend our Eastern frontier. You mind only Kashmir and Pakistan.[3]

Few senior officers would be willing to confront the prime minister again.

Cariappa's was not the only warning that Nehru had ignored. On November 7, 1950, Sardar Patel, a Congress leader, had written Nehru a carefully thought-out letter telling him of the Chinese threat. Although Nehru did not take the note seriously, the General Himmatsinghji Committee was established in February 1951 to look into the defense of the Northeast Frontier Agency.[4] The committee produced an extensive report outlining the military shortcomings in the area and making a series of recommendations, few of which were ever implemented. A paucity of funds, difficult terrain, and the lack of a sense of urgency probably explains this failure. The Better Roads Organization, which the committee recommended, was set up only in 1960.

Nehru continued to believe that the Chinese would not attack, though by the late 1950s he had come to realize that the PRC was a "hostile" state.[5] Still, he did not change his mind about the military.

The nadir for the military services, particularly the Army, came during Krishna Menon's tenure as defense minister (1957–1962). The year 1957 seemed to start off well for the Army: The able and well-liked General Thimayya became chief of the Army staff, and Nehru's close confidant and favorite, Krishna Menon, was made secretary of defense. It seemed like a good team, and perhaps Menon's appointment meant greater attention to the military. Menon, however, had no knowledge of military matters, was accused of procommunist and pro-Chinese sympathies, and shared Nehru's antimilitarism.

[3]Major K. C. Praval, *The Indian Army After Independence*, rev., Lancer International, New Delhi, 1990, p. 143.

[4]Steven A. Hoffman, *India and the China Crisis*, University of California Press, Berkeley, 1990, p. 31. See also Praval, pp. 144–145.

[5]Hoffman, pp. 55 and 221.

General Thimayya warned Indian leaders of the Chinese threat and the weaknesses of the Indian Army, but they ignored him and his relations with the defense minister deteriorated. Thimayya offered his resignation when his relations with Menon developed almost into open warfare. The timing was unfortunate. The next day, General Ayub Khan, the president of Pakistan, was to discuss joint defense policy with the Indians. Nehru talked Thimayya out of resigning. Thimayya hoped that the prime minister might chasten Menon; instead Nehru ridiculed Thimayya in public. Thimayya lost his credibility with his fellow officers and Menon totally ignored him.

Menon wreaked havoc with the Army and caused mistrust and suspicion among the services and between them and the ministry.[6] He was openly contemptuous of and rude to senior Army officers; he often seemed to try to humiliate them; he encouraged cliques, sought to turn juniors against seniors, sowed distrust among the officer corps, and promoted his own favorites. He chose General P. N. Thapur over the Army choice, General Thorat, as chief of the Army staff and made his favorite, General P. M. Kaul, chief of the general staff of the Army.

Menon politicized the Army, a fate it had carefully tried to avoid. It was increasingly demoralized and largely unprepared for the Chinese attack in 1962, which Menon said would not take place. Once the war began, Nehru and Menon tried to micromanage it from New Delhi, though neither had any military experience.[7]

The Indian defeat and humiliation awakened Nehru and India to the fact that the country needed strong military forces. Nehru reluctantly fired Menon, though under him not all had been bad. The Army had established important new schools, one for jungle warfare and one for high-altitude combat. The National Defence College was established in New Delhi. Menon had created new factories for the production of weapons and began to improve military facilities, such as barracks.

After Menon's departure in 1963, the military budget doubled. The Army began a rapid expansion, the Air Force received increased support, and even the Navy received more attention and funds. General Chaudhuri, the new chief of the Army staff, was an able and impressive leader who improved Army morale and supervised the Army's

---

[6]Kadian, p. 52. Major General Rajendra Nath, *Military Leadership in India: Vedic Period to the Indo-Pakistani Wars,* Lancer Books, New Delhi, 1990, pp. 299–303.

[7]See Stephen P. Cohen, *The Indian Army: Its Contribution to the Development of a Nation,* University of California Press, Berkeley, 1971, p. 176.

expansion. He was supported by a helpful and sympathetic defense minister, Y. B. Cheran. India has held to a fairly steady expenditure of between 3 to 4 percent of GNP on the military since that time.

Prime Minister Indira Gandhi understood the need for the military and how to use it. She gave the services ample time to prepare for the campaign against East Pakistan to set up Bangladesh. General Manekshaw, chief of the Army staff, included the other two service chiefs in his plans. Interservice coordination worked well and contributed to the 1971 victory. This triumph restored the confidence of the military and revealed the progress that it had made, and India could hold its head high again.[8] But even after the victory, the military leaders were again lowered in status in the Warrant of Precedence, possibly because Mrs. Gandhi did not want them to become too popular or too powerful.

Civilians have feared a military coup since independence. It is not entirely clear why this is so, as the Indian Army had rarely challenged civilian control under the British and never since independence. The Army may have been considered too pro-British, not in tune with the nationalist times, and hence not entirely reliable. Also, armies of other newly independent and developing countries caused some of the alarm, as most had become deeply involved in their own domestic politics. Even the Pakistani and Burmese armies, with the same British background as the Indian Army, played decisive political roles in these two neighbors of India. In fact, General Cariappa, early on, told the Army sternly to remain out of and above politics. Other Army leaders reiterated this theme.

The fear of a coup has led to extremely close control of the military services at the highest level of the government: The Cabinet Committee on Political Affairs (CCPA), rather than the military, makes the major strategy and military decisions.[9] The civilian minister of defense and his civilian staff receive recommendations from the services, make decisions, and pass on the most important issues to the CCPA for decision. A section of the Ministry of Finance with an office in the Ministry of Defence has a near veto on all expenditures proposed by the services, and an input to recommendations to the Ministry of Defence.

---

[8]The progress was less than it seemed because Pakistani forces were woefully weak, as General Manekshaw knew and admitted. Kadian, p. 63.

[9]This small committee, the pinnacle of government, is chaired by the prime minister and includes the ministers of defense, external affairs, home, transport and communication, and finance; others are invited as needed, including the service chiefs.

The control of unusual major troop movements or other military forces in peacetime resides with the minister. The Ministry of Defence in essence serves as a higher headquarters that makes all decisions; the service chiefs have no statutory power to make government decisions.[10] They are limited to operations and operational plans.

Many of the civilians in Defence and Finance have little knowledge of military affairs and may be rotated in and out, thus providing little continuity or expertise. The military resent the fact that these largely uninformed and inexperienced civilians make all the major decisions.[11] In addition, civilians control the development and production of indigenous weapons in government-owned laboratories and factories operated by the Department of Defence Production. The Department of Atomic Energy, a civilian agency, undertakes all nuclear developments, while the civilian Space Department develops all missiles. The government maintains that both are civilian efforts directed to peaceful purposes; however, it is unlikely that vast sums are spent in these two areas for civilian uses only.[12]

In effect, the services have been downgraded in status, taken out of the national security decisionmaking process, and for the most part kept ignorant of nuclear developments, while the Ministry of Defence civilian staff has grown in prestige and power and controls almost all military activities and programs. At the same time, civilians and police leaders have been upgraded and their pay increased.

The fear of a coup, along with bureaucratic opposition, has prevented the formation of much needed institutions for the coordination of the military services, as well as the development of a national strategy. Civilians, bureaucrats, and politicians alike have consistently opposed creating the position of chief of the defense staff and a joint staff, which most modern nations have and which India needs. The Navy and Air Force fear that an Army general would hold the new position, giving the Army even greater power; many naval and Air Force officers, however, understand the need for the position, which they believe should rotate. The civilian elite are concerned that the position of chief of the defense staff would give an individual a dangerous amount of power and encourage unhealthy ambitions.

---

[10]Conversation with K. Subrahmanyam, Washington, D.C., April 29, 1992.

[11]General Nath (p. 368) wrote that "a mere joint secretary" handed the order to the chief of the Army staff to evict China in 1962.

[12]Raju G. C. Thomas, *Indian Security Policy,* Princeton University Press, Princeton, New Jersey, 1986, pp. 175, 177, 181.

The chairman of the Joint Chiefs of Staff Committee, made up of the various chiefs, with the senior one as chairman, is the normal forum for coordinating the activities of the chiefs. It works well when they get along; their cooperation in 1971 shows how well it can work. Service rivalries and strong personalities, however, do not always promote cooperation. In any case, modern warfare requires much more staff work than the chiefs can themselves conduct; they cannot get into the detailed staff work needed for joint planning and operations. The Defence Planning Committee is intended to fill that need.

Serving officers cannot talk about the operations of the Defence Planning Committee, and outsiders therefore have some difficulty determining what it actually does on a continuing basis.[13] By most accounts, this staff develops plans for the procurement of weapons and equipment and, on an ad hoc basis, works out strategy and plans papers that are sent to the Ministry of External Affairs and the intelligence community for coordination; once a paper is agreed on, it is sent to the defense minister. Most of the push for joint planning comes from the lower and younger levels of the services.

The Defence Planning Committee is extremely small and interservice feelings are strong, all of which limits what it can do even under the best circumstances. Some observers consider it simply a forum for talk; others believe that it undertakes some planning. Most would agree that the present system does not meet the needs of modern warfare, particularly for a country the size of India. India thus has no effective means at present for interservice coordination in peacetime, for the formulation of national strategies and policies, and for the higher direction of war, should it come. The decision to create a National Security Council, made during the V. P. Singh government in 1990, has not been implemented as of mid-1992.

The Army takes pride in its apolitical stand and its support of the civil government and India's internal security. However, the pressure of continual use for internal security and stability is beginning to take its toll.[14] The Army is not trained for police action; it does not want to oppose its own people; and it feels deprived of valuable training for war, its primary mission. Army personnel increasingly believe that the Army is doing too much large-scale internal security, such as in the Punjab and Kashmir. In April 1992, to the displeasure of some

---

[13]Most information is tightly held, and even among those who know, opinions differ as to the committee's effectiveness.

[14]See *Indian Defence Review*, January 1992, pp. 122–123, for current discussions of the repercussions of using the Army to aid the civil power.

opposition politicians, Army Chief of Staff General Rodrigues said that the poor economy and poor civil governance had led to this state of affairs.[15]

Despite the Army's concern over its internal security operations, its conviction that it must do the bidding of its civilian masters, distasteful though at times it may be, seemingly has not weakened. One finds no hint of a challenge to civilian control. However, some observers, including Americans, worry that continual use of the Army for internal security missions could lead to greater dissatisfaction and frustration in the Army and the possibility that it might decide to take matters into its own hands.[16] This seems unlikely in the immediate future, as the apolitical status of the Army and its belief in civilian control remain a strong part of the military culture.

Some Army leaders have been concerned with the present condition of the Army officer corps. General Sundarji, when he took over as chief of the Army staff in 1986, sent a long letter to all officers in which he complained of poor morale and low self-esteem; he attributed these to the influence of opportunistic, sycophantic, and corrupt officers who thought only of themselves and their careers. He also complained of too great an emphasis on officer privileges and comfort.

Other officers have complained that the downgrading of the services has led to the recruitment of less-qualified officers and, consequently, a lowering of professionalism.[17] Some admit that the top Army leadership has failed to maintain high standards. Many officers feel that the leadership should have fought harder to keep the higher place in the Warrant of Precedence and that it failed to adequately warn the government of the danger to the country of constantly downgrading the military.

Despite the perceived slights, the services today seem to have good morale, self-confidence, and professional pride. The Army remains the dominant service and takes particular satisfaction in its long history. Most officers will quickly and proudly tell their regiment, its age, and its achievements, even though many of these were accomplished under British rule.

---

[15]See "Storm in a Teacup," *India Today,* April 15, 1992, p. 7, which indicated that many civilians had said that they agreed with Rodrigues but that he probably should not have said it.

[16]See, for example, F. Tomasson Jannuzzi, *India in Transition,* Westview Press, Boulder, Colorado, 1989, pp. 121–122.

[17]See Nath, pp. 567–572, for a discussion of the present shortcomings of the Army.

The Army fought to support the British empire in many parts of the world and in both world wars participated in combat with great distinction. Since independence, the Army has helped to keep the country together and served as a symbol of national unity. It participated in UN peacekeeping missions in Korea, Gaza, Indochina, Lebanon, and the Congo, all with great distinction and credit to India. It is probably the most experienced army in the world in missions that contribute to international peace.

The Indian Army has continued such British traditions as great loyalty to the regiments, a high sense of professionalism, and of families having served the Army for many generations.[18] The Air Force and the Navy are developing their own traditions, and both new services have confidence in their abilities. They are also less restrained by tradition and often more open to leadership change and social change in their composition.

The services seem to have taken the lead in developing closer relations with the United States, a significant policy decision not normally made by the services. Officials of the Ministry of External Affairs claim that this could not have been done without their support. The civilians in the Ministry of Defence, it is alleged, at least in the beginning did not support this initiative, but they have now come around: witness the visit of Minister of Defence Pawar to the United States in April 1992.[19]

These actions raise the question of the military's seeking a greater role in policy matters. However, Indo-American relations have been improving in many other areas of government; thus, the military did not really make a major policy decision. Furthermore, civilians still hold tight reins on the military.[20]

The military play only a minimal role in decisionmaking on matters of national security. If allowed to, many well-educated and thoughtful military officers could contribute, under civil direction, to the formulation of national strategy and defense plans. The services remain apolitical and adhere strongly to the principle of civilian control.

The need for interservice coordination and the development of a national strategy remains great but unfulfilled. As the world grows

---

[18]See Kadian, pp. 127–142, for a discussion of retained British tradition.

[19]Secretary of Defence N. N. Vohra came to Washington with Pawar and then returned only two weeks later for the third Indo-American Strategic Symposium held at Airlie House, Virginia, April 21–23, 1992.

[20]For example, the government keeps senior military officers under surveillance to observe their actions.

more complicated and India plays a greater role, the requirements will become ever more pressing. Past governmental progress in addressing these problems is not encouraging, though now, as in the case of economic and financial reform, attention to strategic needs may also increase.

5. A NOTE ON NUCLEAR STRATEGY

Strategies for the use of nuclear weapons—not addressed in this study—will undoubtedly influence India's strategic thinking as time goes on. They may have already done so, but the Indian government has neither announced nor revealed a nuclear strategy, and it continues to pursue a policy of ambiguity about its nuclear capability.

All nuclear developments are carried out by the Department of Atomic Energy, a civilian agency, which maintains that it works only for peaceful purposes. Nevertheless, it exercises tight control over all information on nuclear matters. Up to now, the military have been excluded from the program and therefore do not talk about it. However, a very few military officers apparently are now involved one way or another in the program.

One may reasonably conclude that, given India's peaceful nuclear explosion in 1974, China's nuclear capability, and Pakistan's long-time and well-known desire for a nuclear capability, India has not neglected the military aspects of its nuclear program. Its missile program, again conducted by civilians, has produced the Agni IRBM and other missiles, indicating that relatively long-range missile delivery systems are being developed. Officially, these too are for peaceful purposes.[1] Officials sometimes say unofficially that the Agni, if used for military purposes, will carry only conventional warheads, a contention hard to believe, given the cost of the missile and limited lethality range of conventional weapons.

Pakistan's admitted nuclear capability now has probably increased India's efforts. Mrs. Gandhi took the position that India must respond accordingly to any Pakistani developments. V. P. Singh warned in April 1991 that "Pakistan will have to pay a heavy cost" if it gets the bomb.[2] Prime Minister Rao indicated that India would take care of itself.

One hears limited but increasing public discussion on the nuclear issue, and most of it concerns whether Pakistan has the bomb and whether India should have one.[3] Many Indians oppose having a nu-

---

[1]The Agni tests were referred to as a "technological demonstration," and the 1974 nuclear explosion was called "the peaceful nuclear explosion," or PNE.

[2]*India Express,* April 11, 1991.

[3]India rejects both the Nuclear Proliferation Treaty and the proposed five-power talks, but shares the U.S. opposition to proliferation. It resents the implication that

clear capability on moral and other grounds. A few, however, maintain that India should develop a nuclear capability, arguing that it must have nuclear weapons to deter Pakistan and China and to free itself from blackmail by either. Moreover, they say, it must prepare to use them in war if necessary. They also argue that until India has the bomb, other nations will not recognize it as the great nation that Indians believe it to be.

Some say that the military are not interested in nuclear weapons, that they are content with their conventional superiority over Pakistan; others suggest the services might consider tactical nuclear weapons. In any case, either the active military are specifically prohibited from discussing nuclear matters, or they have an understanding with the civilians that they will not speak out on them.

The Indian military simply cannot be unaware of the problem of nuclear war or of the considerable information about nuclear weapons in the world. They have read the enormous open literature on the subject of nuclear weapons, and they have attended military schools in the United States, the UK, and the Soviet Union where these matters are discussed. The fact that the Pakistanis say they have the bomb must make the Indian military think about nuclear matters, at least privately, even if they are prohibited from official discussions.

Retired officers, including General Sundarji, have strongly advocated that India obtain a nuclear capability. At the same time, Sundarji believes that even if Pakistan has the bomb and uses it, India can still absorb the attack and win the war with conventional weapons. According to one Army officer, when General Sundarji was chief, the Army had already begun to develop defensive tactics against nuclear attacks.

In contrast, K. Subrahmanyam, who has written considerably about nuclear weapons, sees the serious dangers of asymmetry in nuclear capabilities.[4] If a neighbor were to gain a nuclear capability, Subrahmanyam argues, Indian civilian and military morale would

---

the United States and the former Soviet Union acted responsibly but that India would not.

[4]See K. Subrahmanyam (ed.), *Nuclear Myths and Realities. India's Dilemma*, New Delhi, 1983–1984, pp. 195–221, for a discussion of the implications of nuclear asymmetry. Former Minister of Defence K. C. Pant also warned of the dangers of asymmetry.

both suffer, though this did not seem to be the case after the public announcement that Pakistan had the bomb.[5]

A nuclear capability, Subrahmanyam said, allows the state that has it to concentrate its forces against a nonnuclear state, which would have to disperse its forces. He further suggested that psychological operations could cause panic in the nonnuclear country, creating huge refugee problems and impeding military operations. These psychological operations, in his view, might succeed so well that the aggressor would not have to use the bomb.

There has been some limited discussion in India of well-known nuclear issues, such as minimum deterrence, a counterforce strategy, and the value of a second-strike capability, but there have been no major studies, at least none that have been made public. The present diffuse public discussion does not help much in understanding Indian nuclear strategy, or ascertaining if it has one.

The PRC has had a nuclear capability for three decades, but this has not caused the Indians to worry greatly.[6] Secretary of External Affairs J. N. Dixit, on a visit to Washington in March 1992, calmly stated that the PRC had tactical nuclear weapons in Tibet. The Indians, he said, have lived with this threat for years. China's huge explosion in June 1992 may change the Indians' casual attitude.

Indians view Pakistan's nuclear capability in an entirely different light from the way they view China's. But even in the case of Pakistan the public has not panicked. Indians have openly discussed this situation, and the public seems assured that the Indian government has it under control.

While some fear the asymmetry problems raised above, others, like General Sundarji, say that this really does not matter so much, though he still urges India to get the bomb. Some argue that it would be better for both India and Pakistan to announce that they have the bomb, as that would create a more stable situation; others argue the

---

[5]Secretary of External Affairs Dixit said at a breakfast in Washington, March 11, 1992, that India has known since 1987 that Pakistan had the capacity to make the bomb.

[6]See IDR Research Team, "Nuclear China: The Equation with India," *Indian Defence Review*, July 1989, for an interesting review of Chinese nuclear capabilities and intentions.

opposite, especially in Pakistan, where the generals control the bomb, unlike in India, where civilians control it.

Based on this analysis of Indian strategic thinking, one might conclude that the Indians may not address the problems seriously until a real crisis arises. On the other hand, if the Indians seriously want a nuclear capability, they must develop a strategy for the employment of nuclear weapons. Some say that a small group of civilians is developing this prerequisite, but the leadership has remained silent on the matter. One might also surmise that Indians may be considering reactive or defensive strategy and tactics to deter an opponent, to stop a major enemy breakthrough, to cut the passes in the Himalayas, or to assist in an Indian counterattack.

The military have not participated in policymaking, but some military commanders evidently may now have instructions on the use of nuclear weapons in war under certain circumstances, though these are sealed until ordered to be opened by the civilian government. This presents an awkward situation, as the military maintain that they are unaware of the program, can make no plans, have received no general guidance for the use of weapons, and no command and control system appears to exist.

The present governmental secrecy, the Indian inclination not to plan ahead, and the deliberate policy of ambiguity make an accurate analysis of the effect of nuclear weapons on Indian strategic thinking and strategy difficult and unreliable at this time, at least to any outsider without intelligence information. In the next year or so, however, the government will probably take some action and perhaps even issue some policy statements. Certainly, there will be more public study and discussion of nuclear strategy, and the United States will want to follow these developments.

BIBLIOGRAPHY

Akbar, M. J., *India: The Siege Within: Challenges to a Nation's Unity,* Penguin, Harmondsworth, 1985.

————, *Nehru: The Making of India,* Penguin, London, 1988.

Altekar, A. S., *State and Government in Ancient India,* Motilal Banarsidass, New Delhi, 1984.

Asian Pacific Defence Reporter, 1991 Annual Reference Edition, December 1990–January 1991.

Asian Pacific Defence Reporter, April 1991.

Azad, Maulana Abul Kalam, *India Wins Freedom,* Sangam Books, London, 1988.

Babbage, Ross, and Sandy Gordon (eds.), *India's Strategic Future: Regional State or Global Power?* St. Martin's Press, New York, 1992.

Bakshi, P. M. (ed.), *The Constitution of India: With Comments,* Universal Book Traders, New Delhi, 1991.

Bandyopadhyay, P., *International Law and Custom in Ancient India,* Calcutta, 1920.

Bandyopadhyaya, J., *The Making of India's Foreign Policy,* 2d ed., Allied Publishers Private Ltd., New Delhi, 1987.

Baranwal, S. P. (ed.), *Military Yearbook 1990-91,* Guide Publications, New Delhi, 1990.

Basham, A. L., *The Wonder That Was India,* Sidgwick & Jackson, London, 1967.

Baxter, Craig, Yogendra K. Makik, Charles H. Kennedy, and Robert C. Oberst, *Government and Politics in South Asia,* Westview Press, Boulder, Colorado, 1987.

Bayly, C. A., *The New Cambridge History of India: Indian Society and the Making of the British Empire,* Cambridge University Press, Cambridge, 1987.

Bhaduri, Major Shankar, and Major General Afsir Karim, *The Sri Lankan Crisis,* Lancer Paper 1, Lancer International, New Delhi, 1990.

Birla, K. K., *Indira Gandhi: Reminiscences,* Vikas Publishing House, New Delhi, 1987.

Bouton, Marshall M., and Philip Oldenburg, *India Briefing, 1989,* Westview Press, Boulder, Colorado, 1989.

Bradnock, Robert, *India's Foreign Policy Since 1971,* Chatham House Paper, published in North America by the Council on Foreign Relations Press, New York, for The Royal Institute of International Affairs, London, 1990.

Brass, Paul R., *The New Cambridge History of India: The Politics of India Since Independence,* Cambridge University Press, Cambridge, 1990.

Brata, Sasthi, *India: Labyrinths in the Lotus Land,* William Morrow & Co., Inc., New York, 1985.

———, *India: The Perpetual Paradox,* Rupa, Calcutta, 1986.

Brines, Russell, *The Indo-Pakistani Conflict,* Pall Mall Press, London, 1968.

Brown, Judith M., *Modern India: The Origins of an Asian Democracy,* Oxford University Press, New Delhi, 1988.

———, *Gandhi—Prisoner of Hope,* Yale University Press, New Haven and London, 1989.

Campbell-Johnson, Alan, *Mission with Mountbatten,* Atheneum, New York, 1985.

Chandra, Satish (ed.), *The Indian Ocean, Explorations in History, Commerce and Politics,* Sage Publications, New Delhi, 1987.

Chaudhuri, Nirad C., *Thy Hand, Great Anarch!* The Hogarth Press, London, 1987.

Chibber, Aditya, *National Security Doctrine: An Indian Imperative,* Lancer International, New Delhi, 1990.

Chibber, Lieutenant General Dr. M. L., *Military Leadership to Prevent a Military Coup,* Lancer International, New Delhi, 1986.

Chishti, Lieutenant General Faiz Ali, *Betrayals of Another Kind: Islam, Democracy and the Army in Pakistan,* Asia Publishing House, London, 1989.

Cohen, Stephen P., *The Indian Army: Its Contribution to the Development of a Nation,* University of California Press, Berkeley, 1971.

—— (ed.), *The Security of South Asia: American and Asian Perspectives,* Vistaar Publications, New Delhi, 1987.

—— (ed.), *Nuclear Proliferation in South Asia: The Prospects for Arms Control,* a report prepared for Los Alamos National Laboratory, Westview Press, Boulder, Colorado, 1991.

Cohen, Stephen P., and Richard L. Park, *India: Emergent Power?* Crane Russak, New York, 1978.

Daedalus, Fall 1989 (entire issue devoted to India).

Das Gupta, Ashin, and M. N. Pearson (eds.), *India and the Indian Ocean, 1500–1800,* Oxford University Press, Calcutta, 1987.

Datta-Ray, Sunanda K., "India's Monroe Doctrine," *The Sunday Statesman,* August 2, 1987.

de Riencourt, Amaury, *The Soul of India,* rev., Honeyglen, UK, 1986.

Dikshitar, V. R. Ramachandra, *War in Ancient India,* Motilal Banarsidass, New Delhi, 1987.

Dunbar, Sir George Bt., *A History of India from the Earliest Times to the Present Day,* Ivor Nicholson & Watson Ltd., London, 1936.

Dutt, Srikant, *India and the Third World: Altruism or Hegemony?* Zed Books Ltd., London, 1984.

Dutt, V. P., *India and the World,* Sanchar Publishing House, New Delhi, 1990.

Embree, Ainslie T. (ed.), *The Hindu Tradition: Readings in Oriental Thought,* Vintage, New York, 1972.

——, *India's Search for National Identity,* rev., Chanakya Publications, New Delhi, 1987.

——, *Imagining India: Essays on Indian History,* Oxford University Press, New York, 1989.

Fischer, Louis, *The Life of Mahatma Gandhi,* Grafton Books, Collins Publications Group, London, 1982.

Fishlock, Trevor, *India File: Inside the Subcontinent,* John Murray, London, 1983.

Gascoigne, Bamber, *The Great Moghuls,* Dorset Press, New York, 1971.

Glazer, Sulochana Raghavan, and Nathan Glazer (eds.), *Conflicting Images: India and the United States,* Riverdale Co., Riverdale, Maryland, 1990.

Goldman, Robert P. (translator), *The Ramayana of Valmiki, Vol. I: Balakanda,* Princeton, New Jersey, 1984.

Griffiths, Sir Percival C.I.E., *Modern India,* Ernest Benn Ltd., London, 1957.

Gupta, Rajni Kant, *Military Traits of Tatya Tope,* S. Chand & Co., New Delhi, 1987.

Haksar, P. N., *India's Foreign Policy and Its Problems,* Patriot Publishers, New Delhi, 1989.

Hansen, Waldemar, *The Peacock Throne: The Drama of Moghul India,* Holt, New York, 1972.

Hardgrave, Robert L., *India: Government and Politics in a Developing Nation,* 3d ed., Harcourt Brace Jovanovich, New York, 1980.

Hoffman, Steven A., *India and the China Crisis,* University of California Press, Berkeley, 1990.

Inden, Ronald, *Imagining India,* Basil Blackwell, Oxford, 1990.

India Today, New Delhi, 1990–1992.

Indian Defence Review, New Delhi, 1986–1992.

Iyer, Nandhini, *India and the Indian Ocean,* ABC Publishing House, New Delhi, 1985.

Jain, B. M., *South Asian Security: Problems and Prospects,* Sangam Books, London, 1987.

Jaisingh, Hari, *India After Indira: The Turbulent Years, 1984–1989,* Allied Publishers Ltd., New Delhi, 1989.

Jannuzzi, F. Tomasson, *India in Transition,* Westview Press, Boulder, Colorado, 1989.

Jones, Kenneth W., *The New Cambridge History of India: Socio-Religious Reform Movements in British India,* Cambridge University Press, Cambridge, 1989.

Kadian, Rajesh, *India and Its Army,* Vision Books, New Delhi, 1990.

———, *India's Sri Lanka Fiasco: Peacekeepers at War,* Vision Books, New Delhi, 1990.

Kar, Lieutenant Colonel H. C., *Military History of India,* Firma KLB Private Ltd., Calcutta, 1980.

Karim, Major General Afsir, *Counter Terrorism: The Pakistan Factor,* Lancer Paper 2, Lancer International, New Delhi, 1991.

Kautilya's Arthashastra, translated by Dr. R. Shamasastry, Mysore Printing and Publishing House, Mysore, 1967.

Keay, John, *India Discovered,* Rupa, Calcutta, 1989.

Khanna, D. D., *Strategic Environment in South Asia During the 1980's,* Naya Prokash, Calcutta, 1979.

Kodikara, Shelton U., *South Asian Strategic Issues: Sri Lankan Perspectives,* Sage Publications, New Delhi, 1990.

Kohli, Admiral H. N., "The Geopolitical and Strategic Considerations that Necessitate the Expansion and Modernization of the Indian Navy," *Indian Defence Review,* January 1989.

Kothari, Shanti, *Applied Politics,* India Institute for Public Administration, New Delhi, 1989.

Kumar, Satish (ed.), *Yearbook on India's Foreign Policy 1990–91,* Tata McGraw Hill Publishing Co., New Delhi, 1991.

Longer, V., *The Defence and Foreign Policies of India,* Oriental University Press, London, 1988.

Mahmud, S. F., *A Concise History of Indo-Pakistan,* Oxford University Press, Karachi, 1988.

Malhotra, Inder, *Indira Gandhi: A Personal and Political Biography,* Hodder & Soughton, London, 1989.

Mansingh, Surjit, *India's Search for Power: Indira Gandhi's Foreign Policy, 1966–82,* Sage Publications, New Delhi, 1984.

———, "An Overview of India-China Relations: From When to Where," *Indian Defence Review,* January 1992.

Marshall, P. J., *The New Cambridge History of India. Bengal: The British Bridgehead. Eastern India. 1740–1828,* Cambridge University Press, Cambridge, 1987.

Mascaro, Juan (translator), *The Bhagavad Gita,* Penguin, London, 1982.

Mason, Philip, *The Men Who Ruled India,* Norton, New York, 1985.

————, *A Matter of Honor: An Account of the India Army, Its Officers and Men,* Macmillan, New York, 1986.

Ministry of Defence, Government of India, *Annual Report 1985–86,* New Delhi, undated.

Misra, B. B., *The Unification and Division of India,* Oxford University Press, New Delhi, 1990.

Moorehouse, Geoffrey, *India Britannica,* Harper, New York, 1983.

Murty, K. Satchidananda, *The Quest for Peace,* Ajanta Publishers, New Delhi, 1986.

Musa, General Mohammed, *Jawan to General: Recollections of a Pakistani Soldier,* ABC Publishing House, New Delhi, 1985.

Nagar, K. S., and Lieutenant Colonel Gautam Sharma (eds.), *India's Security: Super Power Threat,* Reliance Publishing House, New Delhi, undated.

Naipaul, V. S., *India: A Million Mutinies Now,* Viking, New York, 1990.

Nair, Brigadier V. K., *War in the Gulf: Lessons for the Third World,* Lancer International, New Delhi, 1991.

Nanda, B. R. (ed.), *Indian Foreign Policy: The Nehru Years,* University Press of Hawaii, Honolulu, 1976.

Nath, Major General Rajendra, *Military Leadership in India: Vedic Period to Indo-Pakistani Wars,* Lancer Books, New Delhi, 1990.

Nayar, Lieutenant General V. K., *Threat from Within: India's Internal Security Environment,* Lancer Publishers Private Ltd., New Delhi, 1992.

Nehru, Jawaharlal, *The Discovery of India,* 4th ed., rev., Meridian Books, London, 1960.

————, *The Discovery of India,* Oxford University Press, New Delhi, 1982.

————, *India's Foreign Policy,* Government of India, Ministry of Information and Broadcasting, New Delhi, 1983.

Norman, Dorothy (ed.), *Nehru: The First Sixty Years,* John Day, New York, 1965.

Palit, Major General D. K., *War in the High Himalaya: The Indian Army in Crisis, 1962,* Lancer International, New Delhi, 1991.

Palmer, Norman D., *The United States and India: The Dimensions of Influence,* Praeger, New York, 1984.

Pannikar, K. M., *Problems of Indian Defense,* New York, 1985.

———, *Geographical Factors in Indian History,* Baharatiya Vidya Bhovan, Bombay, 1984.

Pearson, M. N., *The New Cambridge History of India: The Portuguese in India,* Cambridge University Press, Cambridge, 1987.

Praval, Major K. C., *The Indian Army After Independence,* rev., Lancer International, New Delhi, 1990.

Press Council of India, *Crisis and Credibility,* Lancer Paper 4, Lancer International, New Delhi, 1991.

Radhakrishnan, S., *Eastern Religions and Western Thought,* Oxford University Press, New Delhi, 1989.

Rao, General K. V. Krishan, *Prepare or Perish: A Study of National Security,* Lancer Publishers Private Ltd., New Delhi, 1991.

Rao, P. R., *Indian Heritage and Culture,* Oriental University Press, London, 1988.

Rao, Ramakrishan, and R. C. Sharma (eds.), *India's Borders: Ecology and Security Perspectives,* Scholar's Publishing Forum, New Delhi, 1991.

Rasgotra, M., V. D. Chopra, and K. P. Misra (eds.), *India's Foreign Policy in the 1990's,* Patriot Publishers, New Delhi, 1990.

Ray, Hemen, *Sino-Soviet Conflict over India: An Analysis of the Causes of Conflict Between Moscow and Beijing over India Since 1949,* Abhinav Publications, New Delhi, 1986.

Rikhye, Ravi, *The Militarization of Mother India,* Chanakya Publications, New Delhi, 1990.

Rowland, John, *A History of Sino-Indian Relations: Hostile Co-Existence,* Van Nostrand, Princeton, 1967.

Sardeshpande, Lieutenant General S. C., *Assignment Jaffna,* Lancer Publishers Private Ltd., New Delhi, 1992.

Sarkar, Bidyut (ed.), *P. N. Haksar: Our Times and the Man,* Allied Publishers Private Ltd., Ahmedabad, 1989.

Sen Gupta, Bhabani, *South Asian Perspectives: Seven Nations in Conflict and Cooperation,* B. R. Publishing Corp., New Delhi, 1988.

Sharan, Vyupakesh, *India's Role in South Asian Regional Cooperation,* Commonwealth Publishers, New Delhi, 1991.

Sharma, Ram Sharan, *Aspects of Political Ideas and Institutions in Ancient India,* 3d rev. ed., Motilal Banarsidass Publishers, New Delhi, 1991.

Sheppard, Eric William, *A Short History of the British Army to 1914,* Constable, London, 1926.

Singh, Lieutenant General Depinder, *IPKF in Sri Lanka,* Trishul Publications, Noida, undated.

Singh, Lieutenant General Harbakhsh, *War Dispatches: Indo-Pakistani Conflict 1965,* Lancer International, New Delhi, 1991.

Singh, Air Commodore Jasjit, *Air Power in Modern Warfare,* Lancer International, New Delhi, 1988.

———— (ed.), *India and Pakistan: Crisis of Relationship,* Lancer Publishers Private Ltd., New Delhi, 1990.

————, *Indo-US Relations in a Changing World: Proceedings of the Indo-US Strategic Symposium,* Lancer Publishers Private Ltd., New Delhi, 1992.

Singh, Air Commodore Jasjit, and Dr. Vatroslav Vekaric (eds.), *Non-Provocative Defence: The Search for Equal Security,* Lancer International, New Delhi, 1989.

Singh, Professor P. K., "Maritime Security of India," *USI Journal,* New Delhi, October–December 1990.

Singh, Sarva Daman, *Ancient Indian Warfare,* Motilal Banarsidass, New Delhi, 1987.

Singh, Major General Sukhwant, *India's Wars Since Independence: General Trends,* Vol. 3, Vikas Publishing House Private Ltd., New Delhi, 1982.

Sinha, N. K., and Nisith R. Ray, *A History of India,* Orient Longman, Hyderabad, 1973.

Sinha, Lieutenant General S. K., *Of Matters Military,* Vision Books, New Delhi, 1987.

Sinha, Sureshwar D., *Sailing and Soldiering in Defence of India,* Chanakya Publications, New Delhi, 1990.

Sisson, Richard, and Leo E. Rose, *War and Secession. Pakistan, India and the Creation of Bangladesh,* University of California Press, Berkeley, 1990.

Spear, Percival, *A History of India, Vol. 2,* Penguin, London, 1965.

Sreenivasan, M. A., *Of the Raj, Maharajas and Me,* Ravi Dayal, New Delhi, 1991.

Subrahmanyam, K. (ed.), *Nuclear Myths and Realities. India's Dilemma,* New Delhi, 1983–1984.

———, *Nuclear Proliferation and International Security,* Lancer International, New Delhi, 1985.

———, "Defence and Security," paper presented on December 30, 1988, at the ICSSR seminar, "India Since Independence," Parliament Annex, New Delhi, December 26–30, 1988.

——— (ed.), *India and the Nuclear Challenge,* Lancer International, New Delhi, 1991.

Subrahmanyam, K., and Air Commodore Jasjit Singh (eds.), *Global Security: Some Issues and Trends: An Indo-German Dialogue,* Lancer International, New Delhi, 1987.

Subramanian, R. R., *India, Pakistan, China: Defence and Nuclear Tangle in South Asia,* ABC Publishing House, New Delhi, 1989.

Tahiliana, Admiral R. H., interview, *Indian Defence Review,* July 1988.

———, "Maritime Strategy for the 90's," *Indian Defence Review,* July 1989.

Taylor, Jay, *The Dragon and the Wild Goose: China and India,* Praeger, New York, 1987.

Tellis, Ashley, "India's Naval Expansion: Reflections on History and Strategy," *Comparative Strategy,* Vol. 8, No. 2, 1987.

———, "Banking on Deterrence," *Naval Proceedings,* March 1988.

———, "New Acquisitions on the Indian Subcontinent," *Naval Forces,* Vol. 11, No. 1, 1990.

———, "Securing the Barracks: The Logic, Structure and Objectives of India's Naval Expansion," Department of Political Science, University of Chicago, unpublished and undated.

Thakur, Janardan, *V. P. Singh: The Quest for Power,* Warbler Books, New Delhi, 1989.

Thapar, Romila, *A History of India,* Vol. 1, Penguin Books, London, 1987.

Thomas, Raju G. C., *Indian Security Policy,* Princeton University Press, Princeton, New Jersey, 1986.

Times of India (Bombay).

Trench, Charles Chenevix, *The Indian Army and the King's Enemies 1900–1947,* Thames & Hudson, New York, 1988.

Tully, Mark, *No Full Stops in India,* Viking, New Delhi, 1991.

USI Journal (United Services Institute), New Delhi, 1980–1992.

Vali, Ferenc A., *Politics of the Indian Ocean Region: The Balances of Power,* The Free Press, Macmillan, New York, 1976.

Vas, Lieutenant General E. A., *The Search for Security: Controlling Conflict and Terrorism,* Natraj Publishers, Dehra Dun, 1989.

Venkateshwaran, A. P., "To End with a Whimper," *Indian Defence Review,* January 1992.

Viswantha, S. U., *International Law in Ancient India,* London, 1925.

Waller, John H., *Beyond the Khyber Pass: The Road to British Disaster in the First Afghan War,* Random House, New York, 1990.

Wingnaraja, Ponna, and Akmal Hussain (eds.), *The Challenge in South Asia: Development, Democracy and Regional Cooperation,* Sage Publications, New Delhi, 1989.

Wolpert, Stanley A., *Tilak and Gokhael: Revolution and Reform in the Making of Modern India,* Oxford University Press, Oxford, 1961.

——, *India,* University of California Press, Berkeley, 1991.

Woodruff, Philip, *The Men Who Rule India, Vol. 1, The Founders,* Jonathan Cape, London, 1965.

——, *The Men Who Rule India, Vol. 2, The Guardians,* Jonathan Cape, London, 1965.